THE KOH-I-NOOR DIAMOND

The History and the Legend

THE KOH-I-NOOR DIAMOND

THE HISTORY AND THE LEGEND

Stephen Howarth

QUARTET BOOKS
LONDON MELBOURNE NEW YORK

First published by Quartet Books Limited 1980
A member of the Namara Group
27 Goodge Street, London W1P 1FD

Copyright © 1980 by Stephen Howarth

Picture research by Susan Lubbock

ISBN 0 7043 2215 3

Printed and bound by
The Garden City Press Limited
Letchworth, Hertfordshire SG6 1JS

Contents

LIST OF ILLUSTRATIONS 7
PREFACE 9
THE OWNERS OF THE KOH-I-NOOR 12

PART ONE: THE PREHISTORY
1 THE LEGEND 15
2 JEWELS OF FAITH AND STATE 25

PART TWO: THE HISTORY
INTRODUCTION 37
1 GARDENS OF THE KINGS 39
2 THE MERCHANT-TRAVELLER 54
3 TRADE'S INCREASE 68
4 THE SHEPHERD-KING 78
5 THE BOY-KING, THE EUNUCH AND THE AFGHANS 89
6 THE LION AND ALL HIS CUBS 100
7 SWALLOWED UP WHOLE 113
8 TOWARDS A GREATER UNITY 126
9 O FUL, TRU UN PERTIKLER OKEAWNT 135
10 A CERTAIN TRAGEDY 147

BIBLIOGRAPHY 153
INDEX 157

To my parents and my grandparents

Illustrations

Colour plates
between pages 80 and 81

Akrura reveals the Syamantaka to Khrishna. Painting from Northern India, 1525 (*Victoria and Albert Museum*)
Babur in the Garden of Fidelity. Mughal, 1508 (*V & A*)
Akbar inspecting the building of Fathepur Sikri. *Akbarnama*, Mughal, 1590 (*V & A*)
Celebrations for the birth of Salim. *Akbarnama*, Mughal, c. 1590 (*V & A*)
Detail of a cotton hanging, early eighteenth century (*V & A*)
Ivory throne and footstool, from *Industrial Arts of the Nineteenth Century* by Matthew Digby Wyatt, 1851–53 (*V & A*)
Indian vases and jewellry, from *Industrial Arts of the Nineteenth Century* (*V & A*)
Head ornament, Delhi, eighteenth century (*V & A*)
The Grand Hall of Audience in the Mogul Palace, Delhi, from *Les Civilizations de L'Inde* by Gustave Le Bon, 1887
The Great Mosque, Delhi, from *Les Civilizations de L'Inde*
The Indian display at the Great Exhibition, from *Comprehensive Pictures of the Great Exhibition* by Joseph Nash (*V & A*)
The State Crown of Her Royal Highness Queen Elizabeth The Queen Mother (*Crown Copyright, Reproduced with the permission of the Controller of Her Majesty's Stationery Office*)

Black and white
between pages 24 and 25

The marriage of Khrishna's parents (*V & A*)
Brahma, Vishnu and Siva, from Volume I of *Indian Antiquities* by Rev. Thomas Maurice, 1796–1806
The temple of Jagannath, from *Indian Pictures* by Rev. William Urwick, 1891
Krishna and Radha adored by the animals. Udaipur, c. 1800 (*V & A*)
Prince Gotama, the Buddha. Gandnara, third to fifth centuries. (*V & A*)
Buddhist temple, from *Les Civilizations de L'Inde*
Battle scene from the *Mahabharata*, 1598 (*V & A*)
Krishna and the Milkmaids (*V & A*)

between pages 40 and 41

Humayun's accession durbar. Early seventeenth century (*V & A*)
Babur receiving ambassadors in a garden, 1528. *Barburnama*, Mughal, 1588 (*V & A*)
Humayun's tomb, from *Narrative of the Indian Revolt* by Sir Colin Campbell, 1858
Akbar hunting, 1600 (*V & A*)
Mogul palace at Delhi, from *Narrative of the Indian Revolt*
Akbar's tomb, from Volume I of *Views in the East* by Captain Robert Elliot, 1833 (*India Office*)
Interior of Mogul palace. (*I.O.*)
Shah Jahan in 1631. Work of Bicheti (*V & A*)
The Taj Mahal, from *Les Civilizations de L'Inde*
Interior of the Taj Mahal, from *The Illustrated London News*, 1851

between pages 56 and 57

Sketch of the Koh-i-noor, from Volume II of *Travels in India* by Jean Baptiste Tavernier, Baron of Aubonne, translated by V. Ball, 1889 (*I.O.*)

Tavernier in 1679, from *Travels in India* (*I.O.*)
Jahangir with Prince Parviz, 1610–14 (*V & A*)
Aurangzeb, unfinished portrait (*reproduced by Courtesy of the Trustees of the British Museum*)
The Peacock Throne, from Volume VII of *Indian Antiquities*
Rosewood and ivory cabinet. Goa, seventeenth century (*V & A*)
European receiving a message while his servants prepare refreshment. Mughal, *c.* 1600 (*V & A*)
A drunken feast. *Hamzah Namah*, 1564–79 (*B.M.*)

between pages 72 and 73

The Old Court House, Calcutta, from *History of Ancient and Modern India* by Francis William Blagdon, 1805 (*I.O.*)
The East India Company's coat of arms, from *Relics of the Honourable East India Company* edited by William Griggs, 1909 (*I.O.*)
East India, House, Leadenhall Street. Line engraving by Watts, published 1800 (*I.O.*)
Bombay Green, from *Oriental Memoirs* by James Forbes, 1813 (*I.O.*)
Nadir Shah. Moghul, mid-eighteenth century (*V & A*)
Mohammed Shah. Moghul, mid-eighteenth century (*V & A*)
The Shalimar Gardens, Kashmir (*I.O.*)
Europeans seated in a howdah. Udaipur, nineteenth century (*V & A*)

between pages 88 and 89

The Golden Temple of the Sikhs at Amritsar, from *Indian Pictures*
Sikh cavalry, from *Narrative of the Indian Revolt*
Ranjit Singh. Sikh, 1855 (*V & A*)
Lord Wellesley, from *British Government in India* by Lord Curzon, 1925 (*I.O.*)
Ranjit Singh's throne *c.* 1800 (*V & A*)
The diamond in its original setting, from *The Illustrated London News*, 1851
Portrait heads by Emily Eden, June 1841 (*I.O.*)
The battle of Gujerat (*I.O.*)
The Darya-i-noor, from *The Illustrated London News*
The battle of Delhi, from *Narrative of the Indian Revolt*

between pages 120 and 121

Thugs of India, from *Indian Pictures*
Lord Dalhousie by G. Richmond (*I.O.*)
Model of *Medea*, from Volume I of *Catalogue of the Great Exhibition*
Erection of the Crystal Palace, from *The Illustrated London News*
Arrival of Queen Victoria and Prince Albert at the opening of the Great Exhibition, from *The Illustrated London News*
Exterior of the Crystal Palace, from *The Illustrated London News*
Chubb's patent diamond case, from Volume II of *Catalogue of the Great Exhibition*
Victoria and Albert Museum, Bombay (*I.O.*)
The crystal fountain, from Volume II of *Catalogue of the Great Exhibition*
Dhulip Singh by J. A. Goldingham (*I.O.*)

In addition to the acknowledgements to the various institutions given above for permission to use illustrations, the author would like to extend his thanks to Naim Attallah and the staff of Quartet Books.

Preface

Koh-i-noor: the name means Mountain of Light. The diamond called the Koh-i-noor is one of the most famous of the Crown Jewels of Great Britain. It is not the largest diamond in the world, nor is it the most valuable, in monetary terms. Whether or not it is the most beautiful is a matter of opinion; but of all existing jewels, it has the longest history in legend, and the most colourful history in fact.

Diamonds are symbols of eternity. The word comes from the Greek *adamas*, meaning unalterable and indomitable. This, and the poetic name 'Mountain of Light', together indicate the reasons for the high regard in which diamonds have always been held: their beauty and their endurance. Diamonds are one of the hardest natural substances in the world, and many of their uses nowadays are for industrial purposes. But for thousands of years previously they were sought for their beauty, and by their rarity became the province of kings.

The Koh-i-noor was found in an Indian mine, probably more than three hundred years ago, and as the fortunes of India have varied in those three centuries, so the Koh-i-noor has changed hands from one conqueror to another. Through the changes, this special diamond has gradually acquired its own particular symbolism. It has meant different things to different people; to many, it has been an emblem of power and conquest and empire. To others, it has represented something more peaceful, and is an image of union, factually and philosophically. Diamonds as fact, symbol and legend are woven inextricably into the paradox of Indian society, simultaneously changeless and ever-changing. This marriage of constancy and variability can be a difficult concept for many Western minds, but it is this very concept which makes the Koh-i-noor a jewel literally beyond price, for the story of the Koh-i-noor reflects the history of the subcontinent of India. It is a turbulent story, sometimes cruel and violent, sometimes peaceful and calm; and it starts not three hundred years ago, but three *thousand* years ago, in India's oldest legends.

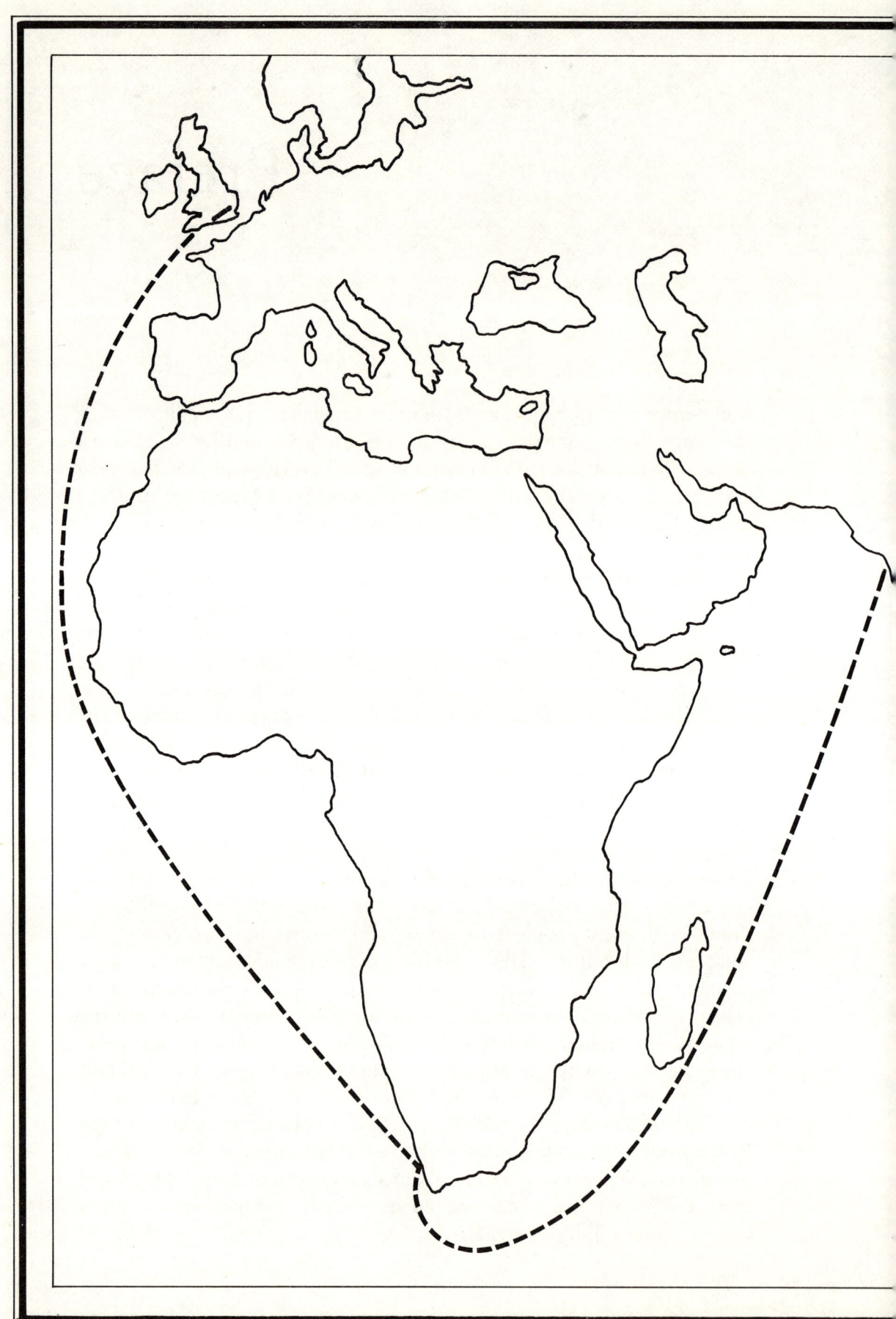

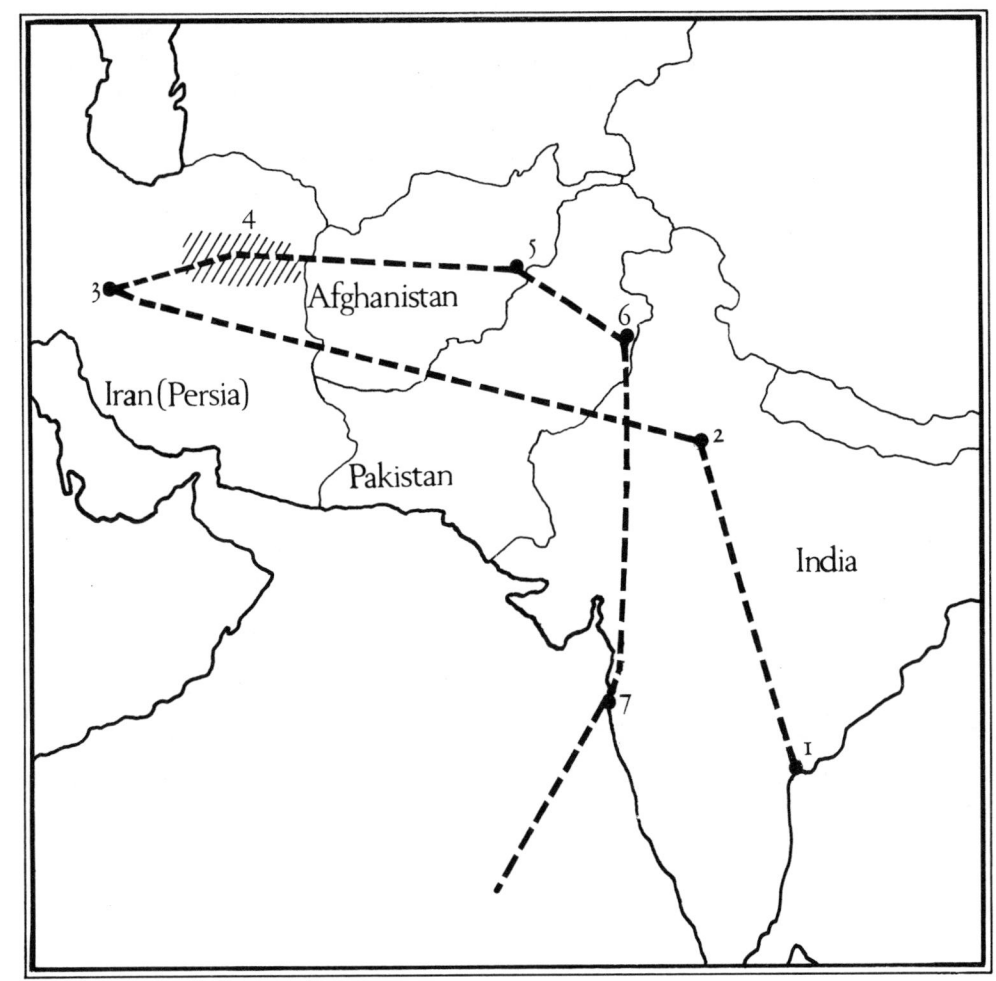

The Route of the Koh-i-noor

1. *c. 1655.* The diamond discovered (in a mine belonging to Mir Jumla) *at Kollur, on the River Krishna in Andra Pradesh.*

2. *c. 1655-7.* The diamond presented to Shah Jahan by Mir Jumla *in Shahjahanabad* (New Delhi).

3. *1739.* The sack of Delhi by Nadir Shah. The diamond is named 'Koh-i-noor' and *goes to Isfahan* in Persia.

4. After being inherited by Shah Rukh Mirza, Nadir's grandson, in 1747, the jewel was given to Ahmad Shah Durrani, *in 1751,* probably *in Khrasan,* northern Persia (Iran).

5. The diamond then went to Kabul *the capital of Afghanistan,* and remained there until *1813.*

6. In that year (*1813*) Shah Shuja at last surrendered the jewel to Ranjit Singh *in Lahore.*

7. On the annexation of the Punjab *in 1849,* the diamond was claimed by the British and *taken from Lahore, to Bombay, to the Cape of Good Hope, to Portsmouth and at last to London, where it remains today.*

The Owners of the Koh-i-noor

MIR JUMLA, one-time wazir to the king of Golkonda, presented it to

SHAH JAHAN, the Mogul Emperor, *c.* 1655–7. It descended to

AURANGZEB, Shah Jahan's son. In 1665 it was seen, weighed and measured by Jean-Baptiste Tavernier, a French jeweller. It remained with the Moguls until 1739, when it was lost to

NADIR SHAH, the Persian emperor, after his sack of Delhi. The jewel went to Persia. After Nadir's assassination in 1747, his grandson

SHAH RUKH MIRZA inherited the jewel. In gratitude for support he gave it to

AHMAD SHAH, leader of the Durrani clan and unifier of Afghanistan, in 1749. The jewel remained in Afghanistan with Ahmad's son,

ZAMAN SHAH, who inherited it in 1793. Zaman was imprisoned and blinded by one of his brothers, but contrived to hide the jewel, until he passed it on to another brother,

SHAH SHUJA, in 1795. Shuja eventually surrendered it to

RANJIT SINGH, the 'Lion of the Punjab', in 1813, in return for military aid. On Ranjit's death the jewel passed to

DHULIP SINGH, his supposed son, in 1839. On the annexation of the Punjab by the British, in 1849, the jewel was claimed by

THE BOARD OF GOVERNMENT, who took possession of it pending its presentation to

QUEEN VICTORIA. The presentation took place on 3 July 1850. Since then the jewel has remained in Britain and is now mounted in the State Crown of Queen Elizabeth, the Queen Mother.

PART ONE

The Prehistory

One

The Legend

The prehistory of the Koh-i-noor begins in the oldest parts of Indian literature, in the books known as the *Vedas* and the *Puranas*. The *Vedas* are records of sacred lore, compiled 1,500 years before Christ's birth; the *Puranas* are collections of myth and legend, the name *Purana* meaning 'Ancient Story'. There are eighteen principal collections in the series of *Puranas*, put together over a period of 1,000 years between 500 B.C. and A.D. 500. These books of lore and legend, whose creation spanned two millennia, tell tales of old gods and new gods – from the first divinities of thunder, sun and rain to the beginnings of the vast and complex Hindu pantheon.

Of the new gods, Krishna was and is undoubtedly the most attractive and the most popular. He was an avatar, or incarnation, of Vishnu the Preserver; his life was such a blend of the human and superhuman, and the aspects of his divinity were so numerous, that ordinary people as well as priests could understand and admire him and, though they might worship different aspects, could also feel united in a common belief. Though Krishna was the nephew of a king, he was brought up as a cowherd, and these diverse social origins, as well as his mischievous nature as a child, his exuberant sexuality as an adolescent and adult, his mature strength and wisdom, and his final calm acceptance of death, made his appeal very broad. The Brahman priests saw the love of Krishna and Radha the milkmaid as the mutual longing between the human soul and the universal soul; less learned people saw it as the fertile relationship of earth and heaven, man and woman, and delighted in the sensual eroticism of the *Gita Govinda*, the love song of Radha and Krishna. Lithe, athletic, merry, Krishna could satisfy an infinite number of lovers; the child-god made every woman the Mother of God; the flute-playing cowherd brought prosperity and fertility to farms and farmers; the heroic leader inspired warriors facing battle; and the subtle, ethical metaphysician could please the priests as well.

In the *Vishnu Purana*, there occurs a legend typical of the many associated with Krishna, in which he is shown as god, hero and a member of the ordinary community. The story is the account of his involvement with the Syamantaka jewel, the gem which hung around the neck of the Sun-god and gave him his brilliance. It is the longest episode concerning jewels in the ancient literature, and it was a popular tale: shorter versions occur through the whole series of *Puranas*. The Syamantaka also shares the typical characteristic ascribed to jewels – it was an emblem of wealth and an amulet for protection and prosperity; and it has been claimed by some hopeful chroniclers to be the legendary original of the present Koh-i-noor. Such a thing is obviously not likely, but the importance of the claim lies in the spirit behind it – the feeling that the diamond named Mountain of Light is an embodiment of the past of the Indian subcontinent, an enduring representation of the country's variety and continuity over centuries and millennia, and a symbol of unity and power.

The sea whispered on the beach as night paled. In the stillness before dawn, there was no other sound. A light breeze, no more than a breath, moved silently over land and water; as silently, a solitary man stood watching the eastern horizon. Slowly, the sky and the far-distant edge of the sea lightened as Dawn approached: Dawn the immortal, ever youthful, ever new, yet old as the earth and the sun in the eternal rhythm of night and day. The man, Satrajit, raised his hands to his chest, palm to palm in an attitude of prayer. As the light grew steadily stronger, his lips moved; in a low and peaceful voice he began to murmur one of the ancient hymns to Ushas, the Dawn, the Child of Heaven.

> 'This Dawn hath yoked her steeds afar, beyond the rising of the Sun,
>   Borne on a hundred chariots, she, the auspicious Dawn, advances
> On her way towards men.
> Shine on us with thy radiant light, O Ushas, Daughter of the Sky,
>   Bringing to us great store of high felicity, and beaming on our solemn rites.
> Mighty One, whom the rishis of old time invoked for their protection
>   and their help,
> O Ushas, graciously answer our songs of praise with bounty and with
>   brilliant light.'

In the clear sky the simple prayer was answered swiftly, naturally, as the red disc of the Sun made its first majestic road across the waters and the evanescent tropical twilight gave way to full day. Satrajit's shadow stretched further behind him as he raised his joined hands above his head in respectful greeting and changed his prayer. Now he sang aloud to the Sun.

> 'His bright rays bear him up aloft, the God who knoweth all that live,
>   Surya, that all may look on him.
> The constellations pass away like thieves, together with their glow,
>   before the all-beholding Sun.
> Swift and all beautiful art thou, O Surya, maker of the light,
>   illumining all the radiant realm.
> Seven Bay Steeds harnessed to thy car bear thee, O thou far-seeing
>   God, Surya with the radiant hair.
> Looking upon the loftier light above the darkness we have come to
>   Thee,
> God among the Gods, the light that is most excellent.'

And then, there on the beach, Surya himself came to Satrajit. The man was dazzled by the god's brilliance; he dropped on his knees and covered his eyes.

'Lord,' he said, 'I have beheld thee in the heavens as a globe of fire; now do thou show favour to me, and let me see thee in thy proper form.'

The Sun-god reached up to his neck and removed the jewel which hung there – the Syamantaka. He put it to one side; Satrajit looked up and saw a dwarfish man with red eyes and a body like burnished copper. Satrajit, if he was surprised, did not show it, but made adoration to the diminutive god, who then offered him whatever gift he should choose. Satrajit chose the Syamantaka.

Surya was true to his word – he presented the gem to Satrajit, then returned to the sky, his brilliance diminished not one whit by the loss. He was a god, after all.

Satrajit put the jewel around his own neck and walked back into his town. Seeing the bright light approaching them, the townsfolk took fright and rushed to tell Krishna that the divine Sun was coming to visit him. Krishna, however, already knew what had happened and calmed the fearful people; Satrajit was made welcome by all.

The new-won treasure not only gave its wearer the radiance of the Sun, but had some very practical side-effects as well. It kept wild beasts at bay, not to mention fire, famine, robbers and evil omens, and every day it produced 1,500 grains of gold. Day by day the townspeople observed the increasing wealth of Satrajit's household. That their town was free of its earlier ills mattered little – that had quickly become an accepted standard. A worm of jealousy grew in their hearts.

Satrajit at the same time was worried, though not by the human intrigue that began to hum around him; whispers and sideward looks did not bother him at all. But he, like the others, was human – Krishna, the incarnate god who walked the same streets, surely had more right to the Syamantaka than a mortal. Might he not claim the jewel as his own? Through long nights made bright as day by the fiery gem, Satrajit pondered, and at last decided to give the Syamantaka away to his brother Prasena.

Had the brothers loved each other better, the transfer might have worked well. Prasena, grim and jealous, accepted the gift with cold pleasure; he knew better than his holy half-wit brother the women and property that gold could buy. With the jewel around his neck, he called for his horse and rode out to hunt lions like a prince. That day's hunt was his last.

Everyone believed a god could be as covetous as a man, and when Prasena did not return from the hunt, the Yadavas – the people of the town – nodded knowingly to one another. No doubt Krishna had followed the hunter and murdered him. Well, they said, smiling slyly and with some regret, we would have done the same; a pity we were not braver. But we dare not attack a god.

Krishna, however, was innocent and indignant. He mounted his own horse and set out on Prasena's track, followed by a group of Yadavas, who were beginning to feel they had been a little rash in their accusations. The tracks, still fresh in the earth, led deep into the forests around the town. Dodging creepers and ducking under branches, the horsemen trotted along, uncomfortably aware of Krishna's anger, muttering at one another for having been such fools.

They caught up with the blue-skinned god in a clearing. Still astride his horse, he was gazing down at a body – that of Prasena, torn and mauled. The spoor of a lion led away from the corpse. The Yadavas dismounted and stood shuffling their feet.

'It was his own evil on him,' Krishna murmured. 'The Syamantaka brings good to good, evil to evil. Some of you take the body back to the town – the others follow me. I shall recover the jewel for Satrajit, who is its rightful owner.'

There was something of a rush to join the returning party. Those who were last followed Krishna again, full of apologies to him. He rode ahead unsmiling.

Very soon the whole group came upon the lion's body. This time a bear's pads led away from it, into a cavern at the foot of a mountain. Krishna instructed the remaining Yadavas to wait for him, and entered the bear's lair.

A week went by, and he did not appear. The Yadavas, in some relief, rode back and announced his death. All the appropriate funeral rites were given, with food and drink being offered to the departed spirit; then, a fortnight later, to everyone's surprise and the delight of most, the man-god returned on foot from the jungle. He was not alone. Apart from the Syamantaka, he brought with him a bride.

The adventures surrounding the divine stone continued for several years. Krishna's new bride was the daughter of the King of the Bears, whom he had defeated in a three-week battle in the cave. Satrajit, despite having the Syamantaka once more, was still worried about Krishna, fearing that the god might bear him a grudge for causing so much trouble. Before long he persuaded Krishna to marry his daughter. The townspeople became even more jealous, and one of the girl's erstwhile suitors murdered Satrajit in his sleep, stealing the Syamantaka after he had done so.

The remainder of the story paints a picture, probably faithful, of the ways of life of the village and small town: the loosely formed self-government of the clans; the rivalries, strife and personal violence that could erupt; the feuds that could ensue; the role of women and the elders in public and private life. In the post-Vedic age, the people of Northern India, inheritors of the Aryans, were in a state of some transition — the power of the old gods had waned, but they were still very much alive in the popular mind; at the same time, the Brahman priesthood, which was to gain power as great as that of kings, had begun to arrogate greater spiritual leadership for itself — and, consequently, ever-increasing material wealth.

After Satrajit's death, the blood-rights of revenge swung into motion with a horrid inevitability. The murderer's jealousy had been fired into action only by promises of support from other forsworn suitors in the event of a feud. Krishna, as Satrajit's son-in-law, was bound to revenge the dead man, and to that end enlisted the aid of his brother Balarama, who was a famous and formidable warrior. Once more the mortals involved began to doubt the wisdom of quarrelling with a god; and the idea of tackling not only the god but also his brother created a general panic. Suddenly the murderer found all his supporters deserting him one after the other. The only thing left for him was flight. Before his escape, however, he managed to entrust the Syamantaka to a man named

Akrura, imposing on oath that its whereabouts would never be revealed.

Learning of the murderer's escape, Krishna and Balarama set out in pursuit, and chased him for 300 miles, he on horseback and they in a chariot. He led them across desert plains and fertile valleys, and tried at last to shake them off by taking to rough ground where the chariot could not travel. Weaving among rocks and stones, struggling through mud and scree, the horse could no longer take the strain; its heart burst. At the same time the pursuing chariot swerved and bounced to a halt on the fringe of the rocky tract, and flight and pursuit continued on foot. Balarama stayed with the chariot; Krishna chased the murderer six miles across country, and at last was close enough to fling his knife edged discus. The flying blade sliced off the man's head.

The Syamantaka, however, was nowhere to be found. Balarama, angry and incredulous, disowned Krishna as a perjurer, despite all Krishna's injured protestations of innocence. The brothers separated in high dudgeon, Krishna returning home and Balarama taking up residence in a neighbouring capital city, where he taught the art of fighting with the mace. It was three years before he was persuaded of Krishna's innocence. Clearly the wish to possess the jewel had played as much part in the chase as had the duty of revenge, and though its whereabouts remained secret, it was not forgotten.

Fifty-two years passed. Throughout that time, Akrura's wealth grew steadily. He had given gold and cows to the Brahmans, who prayed for him; he had distributed alms and lived the life of a devout prince. Neither plague nor famine visited the country, though the inter-family feuds and alliances continued, and it was one of these which occasioned the rediscovery of the stone. A murder was committed by a family allied to Akrura, and to escape retribution he accompanied the family in their flight from the town. As soon as he left, calamities and pestilences began to occur. Krishna summoned the elders of the town to discuss the matter.

The old men scratched their beards and confabulated. At last one of them straightened up as much as he could, came to Krishna and delivered the council's opinion. Akrura's parents, they said, had been particularly blessed people, who gave both cows and gold to the Brahmans; his father's presence in a country had always rendered that country fertile, and his mother had been born under the special care of the Brahmans. Consequently, it seemed to the elders highly likely that the same traits had passed into Akrura, and they urged that he be invited to return – adding, at the same time, a rather revealing comment: *the faults of men of exalted worth*, they said, *must not be too severely scrutinized.*

Krishna had, in all these episodes, displayed a remarkably human lack of omniscience, and it was not until he saw the extraordinary cessation of troubles when Akrura returned that he became suspicious. There was more to this than met the godly eye, it seemed, and he guessed that Akrura had possession of the divine jewel. Suspicion led to a similarly un-godlike subterfuge; Krishna called a meeting of the townspeople at his house to celebrate a religious festival. Akrura was among those present, and while the festivities were going on, Krishna took him aside and charged him with possessing the Syamantaka. Fifty-five years after the theft of the jewel from Satrajit, Krishna's innocence had never been completely established, and he wanted to set the record straight.

Reading the old story, one can detect a distinct sense of relief in Akrura's answer to Krishna. All those years the same fear had haunted him as had haunted Satrajit: namely, that the divine Krishna was more suited to be the owner of such a gem; but Akrura had realized at the same time that the stone was essential to the welfare of the kingdom, and so with great worry and anxiety had kept it. Krishna led him out to the front of the whole gathering, and asked him to reveal the gem to all. Akrura reached into his clothes and drew out a small gold box.

'This,' he said, 'contains the Syamantaka. Let him to whom it truly belongs now take it.' As he opened the little casket, the whole room was lit up by the radiance of the jewel. There was pandemonium – everyone shouted and yelled in delight and astonishment, and Balarama came pushing out of the throng.

'It's mine!' he shouted. 'It belongs to my brother Krishna and me as heirs of Satrajit!' He made a lunge for the box, and as Akrura stepped aside, there came another voice which gave a shrill cry: 'The jewel belongs to me!' It was Satrajit's daughter, Krishna's wife. Faced by the furious pair, Akrura drew back swiftly, clutching the precious stone to his chest, and Krishna at last showed that touch of divinity which lies in conciliation. He stepped into the centre of the covetous triangle, raised his arms and shouted above the din for silence. As the voices all around gradually quietened, he took the jewel from Akrura and then, in the presence of the entire assembly, spoke directly to him.

'Akrura,' said the blue-skinned god, 'this stone belongs both to myself and to Balarama, and it is the patrimonial inheritance of my wife. But I have only wished that it be shown to the assembly so as to clear myself of the charge of its theft, for if it is to benefit the whole community, it must be worn by a virtuous and pure person. Remember Prasena, Satrajit's brother; the stone will cause the death of any impure person who dares to wear it. Now, as I have 16,000 wives, I am not qualified to take care of it. For Satrajit's daughter, who is one of my wives, to take the jewel, she would have to renounce me; she will not do that. As for my brother Balarama, he is much too fond of wine and all the sensual pleasures to lead a life of self-denial. Really, we are all completely out of the running; but you have looked after the jewel well for fifty-five years, and so with the agreement of my wife, my brother and the assembled people, I request you to keep the Syamantaka yet, for the good of us all.'

Everyone did agree; and Akrura wore the holy jewel publicly from then on, suspended from a cord around his neck, and like the sun he moved about wearing a garland of light.

The culture represented by the legend of the Syamantaka was a simple one, of small independent towns linked by blood and local political alliances, based on an agricultural economy. But despite its antiquity and simplicity, it was not the first social organization in the Indian subcontinent. The authors of the *Vedas* and the *Puranas* were Aryans, a race of comparatively tall, light-skinned people who invaded the subcontinent in about 1500 B.C. and destroyed a thriving and complex commercial culture based on the Indus Valley. The twin capitals of the Indus Valley civilization, Harappa and Mohenjo-Daro, each covered a square mile. They were built on a common plan and had many aspects of organized uniformity, even down to the size of bricks. But both were sacked by the Aryans and left to be covered by drifting sand and soil; and despite the material sophistication of the Indus Valley culture, it is the Aryan legacy that has lasted.

The Aryans despised the indigenous people, a shorter, darker race whom they called the Dasyus, *dasyu* meaning 'dark'. The invaders worshipped the natural forces, with Indra, the personification of thunder, as the chief of the gods. He was also the archetypal battle-leader, very tall and enormously strong; he usually fought with bow and arrow from a chariot, as did the Aryans themselves. They were a crude, energetic and vital race, people of the sensual earth, and they knew their position in relation to the gods; the divinities were thoroughly human in their characters, but much more powerful, and could usually be relied upon to deliver the goods – if approached in the right way. Indra, the tall, muscular Thunder-god, had a bushy brown beard and a massive appetite; he would eat vast amounts of food and was often drunk – though his divine status did not save him from experiencing some very human hangovers. Milk and mead were the principal Aryan drinks, beef and bread their principal foods. They loved chariot racing and gambling; their music was played on lyre, lute, flute, drum and cymbal. The society was led and dominated by men; meetings held regularly for village politics and farming chat were exclusively male, and descent was patrilineal, with the main objective of marriage being the production of a son.

In their way, they were a cultured and godly society – the *Vedas* were their offspring. Surya, the Sun-god, was male, but Dawn was a goddess, and she gave inspiration for the loveliest passages of all the *Vedas*.

> Common, unending, is the Sisters' pathway; taught by the Gods, alternately they travel.
> Fair-formed, of different hues and yet one-minded, Night and Dawn neither clash nor tarry.
> Bright leader of glad sounds, our eyes behold her; splendid in hue, she hath unclosed the portals.
> She, stirring up the world, hath shown us riches; Dawn hath awakened every living creature.
> We see her there, the Child of Heaven, apparent, the young maiden blushing in her shining raiment.

The Aryan mind was well aware, too, of the brevity of human life in the context of eternity.

> How long a time, and they shall be together – Dawns that have shone, and Dawns to shine hereafter?
> She yearns for former Dawns with eager longing, and goes forth gladly, shining with the others.
> Gone are the men who in the days before us looked on the rising of the earlier Morning;
> We, we the living, now behold her brightness, and they come nigh who shall hereafter see her.

Gradually, from this sense of things within and beyond the human scale, the Aryans began to grow away from their separate gods and goddesses; the concept of an ultimate unity that was made manifest in many different ways entered philosophical thought. It was during this period, the late Vedic age – the third and fourth centuries A.D. – that the caste system began to emerge, creating the distinctive social pattern that still exists in the subcontinent. For, simultaneously with the beginning of more abstract thinking, came the recognition of four distinct areas of society: the priests, warriors, merchants or peasants, and the serfs – respectively, the Brahmans, Kshatriyas, Vaisyus and Sudras.

The Indian term *varna* is only loosely translated as 'caste', and would be more accurately given as 'colour'; the original social divisions were based on colour, with the Sudras, the dark descendants of the Dasyus and the Dasyu–Aryan marriages, as the lowest. Caste, however, implies purity of race, and that was the original intention of the fourfold social stratification: the maintenance of Aryan racial purity. Initially the caste system was fairly loose, and it was possible for a person to move from one to another; but slowly the priests, in their role of mediators between the divine and the human, took increasing control and began to close the system. Caste was seen as a divine ordinance, a manifestation of the four parts of the Creator, with the Brahmans as his mouth, the Kshatriyas his arms, the Vaisyas his thighs and the Sudras – naturally – his feet. Below the main divisions, the web of sub-caste, fenced about tightly with all manner of taboos, grew unbelievably complicated; its complexity forms the true support of Hindu society. The reason for the priests' rise to dominance in the social order was the fact that none of the sacred hymns was written down; they existed only in the priests' memories, and so a kind of spiritual blackmail developed: deviation from the patterns of sacred lore could bring untold disaster – even when those patterns had become meaningless. The names of the old gods stayed, and they were still worshipped; but in the increasingly abstract Brahman thought, they slowly fell from grace, and there rose in their stead the Hindu trinity – Brahma, the Creator; Vishnu, the Preserver; and Siva, the Destroyer.

The provenance of divinity: Krishna was the child of
human parents, seen here at their wedding

The three aspects of Being in the Hindu pantheon: Brahma,
the Creator; Vishnu, the Preserver; Siva, the Destroyer

The Hindu temple of Jagannath or Juggernaut to which the
Koh-i-noor was nearly presented (see page 112)

left: Krishna and Radha adored by the animals

above right: The tranquility of enlightenment: Prince Gotama, who became the Buddha, with the *urna* (the Third Eye) on his forehead

right: A Buddhist temple

opposite: A battle scene from the epic poem, the *Mahabharata* showing the Pandavas and the Kauravas

A famous incident from the life of the youthful Krishna: the milkmaids implore him to return their garments which he has stolen while they bathe

Two

Jewels of Faith and State

The aura of legend clung for many more centuries, both to the Koh-i-noor and to life in India. The tantalizing vagueness of early Indian records has given factual events of the 600 years before and 600 years after Christ's birth the feeling of legend, and in the same vagueness the Koh-i-noor attained the status of myth. This does not mean myth in the sense of fairytale, but rather myth as symbol; the diamond, indomitable and eternal, began to emerge during this period as a very potent emblem, representing the Indian vision of the unity and eternity of their society.

Much of what we know about this time comes from non-Indian sources, in particular from the records of Greek ambassadors and Chinese pilgrims. Alexander the Great had attempted unsuccessfully to invade India, leaving a legacy of formal and informal representatives, and, by the early centuries of the Christian era, Buddhism had spread widely through China, where many people regarded India as a spiritual homeland. To some extent the egalitarian principles of Buddhism had loosened the stranglehold of caste on Indian society, but Hinduism, growing steadily from Vedic times onward, was still very much the dominant religion. Stories had proliferated around Krishna and the other Hindu gods, and some of these gave the bases for India's two greatest literary epics, the *Ramayana* and the *Mahabharata*.

The *Mahabharata* is the longest of all the world's poems; its shortest version has 88,000 verses, and longer ones frequently run to 100,000 verses. In this epic the story is told of the fierce and bloody rivalry between two families, the Pandavas and the Kauravas, whose struggles for control of a kingdom culminate in a great battle in which Krishna is one of the protagonists. He acts as charioteer for Arjuna, the hero of the Pandavas – it was one of the rare occasions when an army could say quite definitely that it had God on its side. Not surprisingly, the Pandavas won the battle; and their king ended the fight as the possessor of a particularly notable gem.

Yudhisthira, king and eldest of the five Pandava brothers, had already been blessed by the Sun-god in a manner strikingly similar to the blessing of Satrajit. Instead of a jewel, though, Yudhisthira had been given a copper vessel which provided abundant food and inexhaustible wealth – the familiar, hopeful idea of the *cornucopia,* but in an Indian setting. Events with a comparably familiar ring gave Yudhisthira possession of 'that celestial jewel'.

One of the Kaurava leaders, Asvatthama, had been born with a jewel on his forehead. But this sign of distinction seemed to be ill-placed, for he had a treacherous nature, and after the battle against the Pandavas had lasted eighteen days, he conceived a perfidious plan for their destruction. Almost all the Kaurava force had been destroyed, and Asvatthama, lying awake in a forest at night, saw an owl attack a group of sleeping crows. Alone, the owl killed most of the crows, and that same night Asvatthama set out to raid the Pandava camp. Moving silently through the camp, he stabbed, strangled, smothered and decapitated, and finally set fire to the whole encampment. Only seven remained alive after the massacre – the five Pandava brothers, Krishna and a kinsman of his named Satyaki. The survivors pursued Asvatthama; their final battle was fought with weapons given by the gods, and would have ended not only in their destruction but in the destruction of the three worlds, Heaven, Earth and Hell. Fortunately, however, two great sages intervened from Heaven, and the conflict was resolved. Asvatthama had to give up the celestial jewel, and was cursed to wander the earth alone and in silence for 3,000 years. The gem passed to Yudhisthira, and he in turn wore it on his brow.

Indian traditions which identify this gem with the Syamantaka conveniently ignore the discrepancy of their origins; but at this stage such attempted links are unimportant. Links of identity only become necessary when fiction and legend turn to fact, and the Koh-i-noor becomes a historically identifiable stone.

Yudhisthira's gem is said to have remained in the Pandava family for many generations; the next traditional association is the first to have a definite date – 325 B.C. In this year, Porus, the king of the Pauravas and a remote descendant of the Pandavas, defied Alexander's invasion of India. The episode is chronicled thoroughly in Greek texts, but is not mentioned at all in Indian work. Even the name Porus is not Indian, but a Hellenized version of an Indian name – possibly Paurava, the tribal name. That the only Indian to resist Alexander should be completely forgotten by native writers is ironic, the more so when one reads the Greek accounts; in those, Porus and his battle against the invaders are clearly portrayed. Porus himself was a gigantic, powerfully built warrior chief with dreams of creating a great kingdom. By the time Alexander arrived, Porus had crushed several neighbouring principalities and tribes; he was aggressive, ambitious, proud and brave, and had no intention of giving in to Alexander without a good fight. Many of the other kings and princes whom Alexander met had surrendered without a murmur, offering allegiance the moment the world-conqueror appeared at their frontiers. Porus, in sharp contrast, announced he would meet Alexander at the frontiers of his land – in arms.

The two armies confronted each other across a wide river; for several days they remained facing one another, observing and manoeuvring. Porus waited for Alexander to make the first move; Alexander made it, taking a force of 11,000 men across the river at the least expected place and time – at a point many miles below the Indian prince's army, when the river was swollen with the winter rains and ran wide and tempestuous. A detachment of 2,000 horse was sent from Porus' camp to delay the invaders; the Indian force was swamped. The European army contained men of many lands, and their vanguard was formed of men from the steppes of central Asia, archers on horseback. This cavalry was the key to the Indian defeat. Porus assembled his elephants in a formidable array, he himself taking the central position on the largest. The elephants were flanked by cavalry and foot-soldiers; but well-trained as they were, the elephants' use was only in the initial dismay of the enemy. The Greek archers, swift and light, soon terrified the elephants with their showers of arrows; the creatures panicked, and in the confusion trampled Indians and Greeks indiscriminately. At last Porus was brought to Alexander to acknowledge defeat. The Indian had received nine wounds and could barely stand; but when Alexander asked him what treatment he should receive, he replied: 'Treatment of a king that it befits a king to give.' Alexander, always something of a romantic, found the reply appealing; he reinstated Porus as king in his former position, and Porus, in his turn, gave allegiance to the Greek.

The main reason for the lack of comment on these episodes in Indian literature is that they made very little impression on India as a whole. Alexander's conquest was quick and unconsolidated; the Greek forces left almost as soon as they had received homage, and they never advanced beyond the Indus. But, indirectly, they paved the way for India's first unity – the empire of the Mauryas.

> I came to Pataliputra: the capital city of Chandragupta Maurya, a large and busy town, fortified and prosperous. Northwards of the city flows the Ganges, and to the west is the confluence with the river Son. The plan of the city is an enormous rectangle, over nine miles

long and nearly two miles wide; there is a high wooden palisade all round it for defence – archers stand concealed beside loopholes in the battlements. The wooden wall in turn is surrounded by a great ditch, sixty feet deep and two hundred yards across – an unpleasant place, for it is the public sewer as well. But the bridges are frequent, and lead to sixty-four gates into the city.

Megasthenes the Greek left this summary description of Chandragupta's capital. He did not speak the native tongues, and had to transliterate names as best he could; Chandragupta became Sandrocottus, Pataliputra became Palibothra, the Brahmans became Brachmans. He had been sent as ambassador to the court of Chandragupta by Seleucus Nicator, a general of Alexander's, who had remained in control of Alexander's Asian conquests and, after the conqueror's death, had welded them into an empire of his own. Although Megasthenes stayed in Pataliputra for a long time, his account of Indian life was not based solely on the Mauryan court; his fragmented records are all of things which struck him as peculiar in the country as a whole. Often he relied on the stories and reports of others, and so there are many excursions into fantasy in his information. He speaks quite seriously of ants as large as foxes that dig gold; of men whose ears are so large that they sleep lying on one and covered by the other; of a river where everything sinks and nothing floats at all; and of people without mouths, who live on the smell of apples, and are killed by noxious odours. But such imaginative ideas were typical of the general Western notion of the fabulous land of India, and if Megasthenes was damned by some later writers as being the second biggest liar of all the Indian historians – the worst being a man named Ktesias – nevertheless, in his own personal observation, he was generally accurate, and his work *Ta Indika* became a standard source of early European knowledge of India.

Chandragupta had come to power in Alexander's wake: the death of the Greek left a political vacuum in the north-west, and having overthrown the ruling Nanda family in the Ganges plain, Chandragupta rapidly acquired an extensive empire, covering both the plains of the Ganges and Indus and the north-west provinces as well. His rule was centralized and tightly controlled; the massive revenues he collected are indicated by the size of his regular standing army – 600,000 foot-soldiers, 30,000 cavalry and 8,000 elephants, all maintained at royal expense. This was the first time that such a large part of India had come under the sway of one ruler, and it laid the first practical roots of the dream of unity that has haunted Indian thought ever since.

The concept of a single king ruling the land from ocean to ocean, an emperor with other kings subject to him, was not new. Yudhisthira, the legendary king of the Pandavas who had acquired the 'celestial jewel', was called a *digvijayin* – conqueror of all the four quarters – and both Kauravas and Pandavas claimed descent from a common ancestor, Bharata, who was said to be the first Universal Emperor. The idea of the Universal Emperor, the *chakravartin*, may have been brought into India by the Aryans, who must have been well aware of the great Mesopotamian powers. At any rate, it was well established by the late Vedic times; and it became an important factor in the growing myth of the diamond, for the emblem of a Universal Emperor was his 'Seven Gems'.

The first of these was the 'Golden Wheel', a many-layered symbol: it represented the cycle of eternity; the embracing temporal power of a *chakravartin*, encircling the earth; and, in Buddhist terms, it stood for the Wheel of the Law, whose instrument and instigator the *chakravartin* was. The other six gems were the 'Horse', the 'White Elephant', the 'Jewel Maiden', the 'Divine Guardian of the Treasury', the 'General Who Could Not Be Defeated', and the 'Jewel That Wrought Miracles'. In practical terms, these were less grandiose; the Jewel Maiden has been interpreted as being the chief queen, the Divine Guardian as the chief minister – generally a priest – and the insuperable General seems to have been an optimistic title for the crown prince. The White Elephant represented power and rank; its colour was valued partly as a symbol of purity, and partly simply because it was rare. The Horse was also a straightforward image of power and high rank; no doubt a particularly fine beast would be chosen for the role. It was also connected with the *asvamedha*, the horse sacrifice, which could only be performed successfully by a Universal Emperor. In this a consecrated horse was allowed to roam freely for a year, all those whose territory it crossed being compelled either to fight or to accept the rule of the king who had freed the horse. At the end of the year, the horse – if it had not been captured by a neighbouring army – was duly sacrificed.

The last of the Seven Gems, the 'Jewel That Wrought Miracles', unlike the others, has no parallel in practical terms; there is no surviving description of it and there may never have been one. But it seems likely that the traditions of celestial jewels from the *Puranas* and the *Mahabharata* were still very much alive; and since the king was accorded divine status, it was natural that the divine gem, the producer of wealth and well-being, should be a part of his regalia.

There was a further secular addition to the myth of the diamond; the image of jewels as things of value and permanence was used in ordering the court's administration. The centre of government was the king himself; around him he had a group of ministers, advisers and other influential people, and these were known as his *ratnins* – his jewels. Their number varied between twelve and sixteen, and a simple list of them clearly shows which social and courtly roles were considered most important.

Foremost was the Purohita, the chief priest and sacrificer for the king. He was closely followed by the Rajanya, a member of the Kshatriya class of nobles; Rajanya was a general caste term, signifying a man of kingly family. The precedence of these first two varied, depending on the piety or worldliness of the king. The king by custom was allowed four wives; the next *ratnin* was the Mahishi, his first wife, followed by the Vavata, his favourite wife, and the Parivrikti, his 'discarded' wife. Presumably these roles were to some extent interchangeable. Then came the king's charioteer; the commander of the army; the chamberlain; the treasurer; the tax-collector; the superintendent of gambling; and finally the village headman. The basic unit of administration was the village, and the Gramani – the headman attending court – probably presided over the village or town where the court was staying. The list was sometimes extended to include the huntsman, courier, carpenter and chariot-maker, but in the more developed society these were hardly likely to have influenced the king in the same way as the other 'jewels'.

The myth of the diamond grew in spiritual life as well. While the fragile magnificence of the temporal court was sustained by the twelve *ratnins* and exemplified by the 'Seven Gems', Buddhism used the image of the eternal jewel to point the way beyond eternity.

Prince Gotama, who became the Buddha – the Enlightened One – was born into the Kshatriya caste, 563 years before Christ's birth. At his conception, his mother Maya – whose name means illusion – dreamed that she was bathed by the guardians of the universe, and that a white elephant holding a lotus flower then entered her womb. This was interpreted to mean that her child would be either a Universal Emperor or a Universal Teacher. A further sign of this destiny was that when the child was born, he took seven steps towards each of the four corners of the earth. Naturally the child's father, as a ruler himself, wanted the prince to become a Universal Emperor, and Gotama was raised to rule. But he was not satisfied, and when he was twenty-nine, he forsook his father's palace and the training meant to lead to the imperial throne. He left behind him a wife and new-born son, and began a life of asceticism that was to last six years. At thirty-five, realizing that asceticism was getting him nowhere, he came back to a rather more normal life and entered on forty-nine days of meditation, which culminated in his enlightenment: he understood the causes of pain, the means of its removal, and the interrelatedness and unity of all life. The rest of his days – his last earthly life – were devoted to teaching. He did not propose himself as a god, nor did he propose any being, seen or unseen, with any attribute whatsoever, as God. It was largely because of this that the powerful Brahman caste allowed his teaching to proceed, for at first it was not apparently in any opposition to them. It was a non-religious, ethical teaching, based on rejection of extremes and acceptance of the 'Middle Way'. Yet it was anything but a teaching of mediocrity – it aimed at heights so far beyond the caste-bound life of the highest Brahman, the Brahman could not conceive them. If he did conceive the freedom of enlightenment, he was Buddhist, though he might remain a Brahman in name. The teaching was classless, open and free to all, and supremely tolerant – it is not surprising that it should have spread widely and rapidly through India, and far beyond, to Ceylon, Siam, Burma, Korea, China and Japan.

Three jewels supported its converts on their way to the innocence on the other side of eternity: the three tenets of faith, the *Triratna*. Privately or in a group, before meditation, work or worship (which are often the same thing), the Buddhist repeats: 'I go to the Buddha for refuge; I go to the Doctrine for refuge; I go to the Order for refuge.' Enlightenment, the goal itself, was exemplified as a jewel in the mantra – the sacred saying, *Om mane padme hum*. Translated as best they may be, the words mean, 'Hail to the Jewel in the Heart of the Lotus'; it is a formula which can take the finite mind as far as possible in contemplation of the infinite. The lotus, India's best-loved flower, represented all material beings; the jewel at their heart was the image of the original and final creative and destructive energy, the simultaneous union and differentiation of every animate or inanimate object.

Images of Buddha often show him with a jewel on his forehead, between his eyes. This is the *urna*, the Third Eye, which sees the light of knowledge. Presumably the jewel which graced the forehead of Asvatthama performed a different function – it is diverting to speculate on the matter: perhaps his gem was more akin to the gem reputed to nestle on the forehead of the toad, a compensation for extreme ugliness. The jewel on Buddha's forehead, at any rate, is the apotheosis of the myth of the diamond. Going further even than the human conception of India's unity in terms of culture, nationhood and living tradition, it stands for the superhuman conception of universal unity.

Although the *Triratna* all refer to 'refuge', Buddha's teaching was never meant as an escapist doctrine; its intent was always realistic and practical. For those who did not achieve enlightenment in their current incarnation, Buddhism still gave a sensitive, balanced and eminently reasonable way of life; and once, at least, this became the announced way of life of an Indian ruler.

Under the benevolent despotism of Asoka, the grandson of Chandragupta Maurya, India came closer than ever before in historic times – and perhaps than ever since – to realizing the dream of complete national unity. Asoka reigned from 273 to 232 B.C. During the first nine years of his reign he extended the empire he had inherited, and the expansion culminated in a war against Kalinga (now Orissa), which was the last independent state in the Bay of Bengal. The emperor himself recorded that in the campaign 100,000 people were killed and 125,000 taken captive; priests, monks, old people and children were murdered. There is no reason to doubt the report, for Asoka was not boasting; he was horrified by the wide and indiscriminate slaughter he had released. His reaction was to become converted to Buddhism; two years later he was ordained as a monk, and he spent the remaining thirty years of his reign propagating Buddhist morality with great vigour, himself, as monk and emperor, providing a very good example. The Edicts of the Emperor were monumental works of inscription, carved into natural rock-faces or on to specially erected pillars throughout the empire; their texts were moral injunctions composed by Asoka, and often have an engagingly simple and personal style. Here is one, in which the emperor calls himself by the typical title of 'Piyadisi, dear to the gods'.

> The kings who were in the past wished thus: 'How may the people grow with the growth of piety?' The people, however, did not grow with a proper growth in piety.
> In this matter thus says king Piyadisi, dear to the gods: 'This thought came to me: I will publish precepts of piety, I will inculcate instructions in piety; hearing these, the people will conform, will be elevated, and will grow strong with the growth of piety. This I did and with the same object also, banyans were planted on the roads to give shade to cattle and men; and at each half-koss wells were dug; also resthouses were made; many watering-stations also were made in this and that place for the comfort of the cattle and men. Little indeed is mere comfort; but, whatsoever good deeds have been done by me, thereto the people have conformed, and those they copy.'

The phrase 'In this matter thus says king Piyadisi' crops up again and again in the texts of the Edicts – generally at the beginning of every paragraph. The sincerity of the man is apparent; Asoka was not a subtle thinker, and it is easy to imagine him dictating to a scribe – perhaps seated on his wide throne, perhaps striding around as he searches for the right word; probably rather pleased with himself when he lists his good deeds, and deeply serious when he adopts a moral tone.

After his conversion, Asoka's united India lived under a banner of tolerance to all – to different sects, different races and different classes. Asoka died peacefully after a reign of forty-one years; the chronic separatism of tribes, clans, nations and states within the subcontinent could only be overcome by a benevolent tyranny.

Throughout the formative centuries of Indian culture, the diamond had appeared in various guises – from the divine gift of riches and well-being, to the homely image of the village headman advising the king and linking court with country, and beyond both gods and men to represent a total unity inconceivable to the intellect. Wherever it appeared, it stood for something that all levels of society shared. A Buddhist pilgrim from China, Hiuen Tsiang, told an apt little story.

> Beside the King's palace stands a shrine some hundreds of feet high, bright and beautiful with precious stones, containing a Tooth of the Buddha; and beside this temple is a small one with a life-size image of the Buddha in gold. The Third Eye of this image was adorned with a valuable diamond before now, until a common thief removed it. He was unable to take it by force, but he entreated the Buddha so earnestly for it, the image bowed down its head, and gave up the jewel to the thief.

Kings, thieves and holy men: the diamond was their common property.

PART TWO

The History

Introduction

Empires, like everything else, have discernible life-spans. Without Asoka's benevolent tyranny, the Mauryan Empire gradually faded. Over the next 1,000 years, only two notable political unities emerged: in the fourth century A.D., there was a second Gupta dynasty in the north – it had no connection with the great Chandragupta, but attempted to steal some of his glory by taking his name. Then, between the seventh and eleventh centuries, most of southern India was ruled by the Chola dynasty.

After the decay of the first, great Mauryan Empire, the intangible patriotic ideal – a nation united from coast to coast under a *chakravartin* – had given way to the more concrete attraction of personal rule of a kingdom, however small. This factor combined with a growing complacency, a conviction that Hinduism and Hindu society were basically superior to any other states; so, by the tenth century A.D., northern India was wealthy, weak and divided.

Exactly 1,000 years after the birth of Christ, the Moslem armies of the Emperor Mahmud of Ghazni entered India for the first time. They came from the north-west, 30,000 cavalry pouring through the narrow passes, lured by the promise of inestimable riches stored in the Indian temples. Mahmud rode as a holy warrior, taking the one true faith of Islam to the infidels of Hindustan; in the previous year, A.D. 999, he had been given the title of 'Defender of the Faith' by the Caliph of Baghdad, and had vowed to go annually to India to propagate his religion. He did not achieve the letter of his vow; but, in the thirty years remaining to him, he invaded India seventeen times.

Islam was a young and vigorous religion, dominating a very large area – from Spain through Egypt and Arabia, and on to Turkestan – and consciously driven by the ideal of a Moslem world-state. It was aggressively egalitarian, recognizing only one God and regarding any representation of God as a sin; to give any attribute to the divinity could lead very easily to idolatry. In striking contrast, Hinduism was defensive and largely concerned with maintaining the *status quo* within its existing boundaries. Polytheistic, conservative, enervated and internally factious, it had lost the vital unity and energy of earlier days, and was a natural prey for the expansionist policy of the new religion.

Within the ranks of Islam, however, there was already one basic division, though only four centuries had passed since the death of the Prophet. Of the two sects, the Sunnis represented the Turkish view, giving spiritual and temporal leadership to the Caliph. The Arabic view, shown in the Shiite sect, held that descent should have been through the immediate family of the Prophet. Mahmud was tenaciously Sunni, at least in part from practical political considerations. Although he was in real terms independent, technically he owed allegiance to the Caliph, and to have the moral support of the suzerain of the Moslem world was no mean asset. His attacks on India were more in the nature of extended raids than actual invasions, for his imperial dreams always looked towards Turko-Persian unity; and though he bore the stamp of a holy warrior, he was not a proselyte. To him, as to many before and since, the crusading flag was an extremely good excuse for fabulously profitable aggression.

Mahmud's era was brief, but it had a lasting effect on the Indian subcontinent; Moslem and Hindu had encountered each other. Over the ensuing years, India *was* united under one rule again, centred on Delhi – but the rulers were Moslem Turks.

The Turkish Sultanate of Delhi began in 1206 with the accession of a former slave, a general in the Turkish armies whose raids had succeeded those of Mahmud. From its origins, this dynasty was known as the Slave Dynasty. Rule of the Sultanate continued under four further dynasties – the Khaljies, the Tughluqs, the Sayyids and the Lodis – and, as a political entity, the Sultanate survived until 1526. Throughout its existence it was subject to the typical vicissitudes of dynastic rise and fall, its boundaries expanding and contracting as the ancient cycle of invasion, conquest, rule, decadence and defeat was played out time and time again. Moreover, the three centuries of the Sultanate were characterized by a perpetual tension between Moslem and Hindu, Turk and Indian; yet it would be misleading to see the flavour of life at this time as one of unmixed opposites, like oil and vinegar. In theory, Moslem politics aimed at the humiliation of the idolatrous Hindus; in practice, the Turkish Sultans frequently found it more expedient to tolerate the religious idiosyncrasies of their subjects.

Nevertheless, after 300 years, the Hindus were chafing under Turkish rule. As Hindu patience wore away, the Sultans became less tolerant, more tyrannical. Then, in the first quarter of the sixteenth century, a new race entered India: the Mongols from Kabul, under their king, Babur.

One

Gardens of the Kings

The advent of the Moguls – Babur and Humayun – 'Babur's diamond' – Akbar, the Universal Emperor – his new religion – the cultural synthesis of Hinduism and Islam – Shah Jahan – Mir Jumla and the 'Great Mogul' diamond

Babur was a gardener. He knew the harmony of growing things; he loved the music that water can make, and filled his gardens with fruit-trees, flowers, pools and streams. From high levels to low ones, the fluid song made a subtle undertone to every part of the melody of the garden, running through stone channels cut in patterns of circles and spirals. Trees would protect the conduits from the sun's heat, and their fluttering shadows played a visual counterpoint, dappling the ripples and sparkles below. His gardens brought out peace in Babur; he would take a book there to study other men's thoughts, or in the quiet of evening would simply stroll beside the grapes and musk-melons, charmed into tranquillity by their light perfumes and the delicate dust that lay on their skins. Sometimes he would stop to savour the cool freshness of the fruit; and sometimes, in the shaded calm, he would think of his wars and conquests, for though his love was given to the natural world, he was by profession a king, a general and a conqueror.

He was a descendant of two of the greatest conquerors that Asia had seen – Tamerlane on one side and Genghis Khan on the other. From Tamerlane's side he had inherited a tiny kingdom at the age of eleven; and it was in the little realm of Farghana, in the north of India, that he learned to love organic life. Farghana was prodigiously abundant in its fruits: pomegranates, melons, apricots and grapes grew with tulips, roses and violets. In wildlife and livestock there were cattle, sheep, goats, deer, pheasants and hares. But though it was pastoral, the kingdom was not peaceful. It was surrounded by minor kingdoms and principalities, most of whose rulers claimed descent one way or another from Tamerlane, and most of whom intended to re-establish Tamerlane's empire, with its fabled capital of Samarkand. Babur had exactly the same idea, and when he was only fourteen he led his army to besiege the ancient city. He won it, after a siege of six months, and then before he was fifteen he lost it again; and within the next fifteen years the same thing happened twice more.

For decades the conquest of the throne and city of Samarkand, which Babur regarded as his ancestral right, had been his sole ambition. He went through astonishing rises and falls of fortune pursuing this dream, sometimes commanding armies of several thousand, sometimes living penniless with shepherds and a very few followers. Not until he was thirty-six did he finally give up the dream and turn his eyes towards Hindustan. He took off towards the south from a new kingdom, having lost Farghana and then, in 1504, taken Kabul.

A picture of him at this time shows him in one of his favourite gardens in Kabul, the Bagh-i Vafa. He had been most impressed by the gardens of Samarkand, and was determined to create similar beauty wherever he might go. In the picture he stands at the corner of a flower-bed, a serious-looking figure in a long yellow robe, pointing out the place for a new flower to be planted. He wears a white turban and red pointed shoes with curling toes; behind him stands a servant with a fan, and before him his men dig, measure and irrigate. Water, the ever-present melodious blood of the earth, runs in channels between the beds and tumbles into a tank. The garden is walled, with fruit-trees growing against the brick; birds swoop and dart above the men's heads; one alights on a tree and looks out, cautiously inspecting the fruit. The men, all turbanned, wear the long frock-like Turkish clothes in red and green, golden, pink, purple and blue; some, newly arrived, salute the king; another bends double over his work; another, behind Babur, stands with a pensive air as though he does not quite agree with Babur's garden plan. It is a colourful, tranquil and very ordered scene, and Babur, the focus of attention, commands it with the same precision and authority with which he might command a battle.

But the stern countenance of the commander is replaced in another portrait by an expression far more typical of the man; this time he holds a book, and on the thin, bearded face there is an attractive look of mild amusement, the product of a light-hearted, good-humoured nature. In fact Babur is one of the most attractive characters in the tale of the Koh-i-noor; the sophistication of the Turk mingled in him with the adventurous nature of the Mongol, and produced someone who, besides being an excellent general, was also a man of culture and sensitivity, and a very good writer. His *Memoirs* stand in a class of their own, a delightful presentation of people and events, mixed with reports of battles, comments on literature, quantities of records of plants and

Humayun's accession durbar held at Agra in 1530 – four years after the event

Babur receiving Uzbeg and the Rajput ambassadors in his garden named Kabul, beside the Agra (see page 44)

The beginning of the union of Indian and Islamic architecture: Humayun's tomb near Delhi (see page 46)

The tomb of Humayun's son, Akbar, at Sikandra, as seen in 1831

left:

Akbar, the 'inventor' of India, hunting

below:

After the gardener came the builders: the Mogul palace at Delhi, from the Jumna

A detail of the interior

Shah Jahan, 'King of the World', in 1631, aged forty

The exterior of the Taj Mahal, at night

By the nineteenth century, India had completely captivated the European imagination. This engraving of the interior of the Taj Mahal appeared in *The Illustrated London News* in 1851

animals, stories of chases and escapes across snow-bound mountains – all related with immense candour and clarity, so that the personality and temperament of the emperor emerge with extraordinary vitality.

On one of their innumerable marches, he and his men became utterly lost in deep snow. It rose above the stirrups of their horses; the travel was exhausting; and then, at nightfall, they found a little cave. Babur himself dug down through the snow breast-deep without finding the ground. He decided to shelter in the hole, though his men begged him to go into the cave; 'but I would not. I felt that for me to be in warm and shelter and comfort while my men were in misery and distress, was not to do my duty by them.' He stayed in his little hole till he had four inches of snow on his head and face; and then it was discovered that the cave was big enough to hold everyone. 'Those who had any eatables, stewed meat, preserved fish, or anything ready, brought them out; and so we escaped from the terrible cold and snow and drift into a wonderful safe, warm, cozy place, and refreshed ourselves.'

Obviously such a sharing attitude endeared him to his men; and other touches of an equally human sort added to their loyalty. After years of total abstinence in his youth, Babur had taken a great liking to wine.

> About the time of noon-day prayers, I mounted to take a ride, and afterwards going on a boat, we had a drinking-bout. We continued drinking in the boat until bed-time prayers, when I was miserably drunk; and next morning, when they told me of our having galloped into camp with lighted torches in our hands, I had not the slightest recollection of it.

But comradeship, generosity and humanity were not the only qualities that drew men to Babur; he had inherited the mystique of the family of Tamerlane, and from the time that he conquered Kabul, the people of the surrounding countries – always responsive to charismatic leadership – began to see him not as one of a multitude of princes with equal claim, but as the sole legitimate heir to the house of Tamerlane. In fact he was the sole heir; by that time all others had been defeated by Shaibani Khan, the chief of the Uzbeg tribes.

Thus it was that Babur rose from being one of the warring princelings to a position from whence he could challenge India; and if he finally lost the hope of re-creating Tamerlane's empire, he more than made up for it by laying the cornerstone for the longest-lasting and most brilliant of all the Indian empires, the empire of the Moguls.

Babur's first incursion into India came in 1519, when he advanced as far as Bhira, on the banks of the river Jehlam – a tributary of the Indus. It was only a raid of reconnaisance, and during the following seven years he entered the subcontinent four times more. The final attack, in 1526, had the singularity of being by invitation. The Delhi Sultanate was tottering under the despotic rule of Ibrahim Lodi; provinces around Delhi had declared their independence; and almost simultaneously, an uncle of Ibrahim Lodi and Daulat Khan, the newly independent governor of the Punjab, came to Babur to ask his assistance in a war against Ibrahim. Babur needed no second bidding.

By the time Babur got to Dibalpur, which lay somewhat south of Lahore, Daulat Khan had changed his mind, however. It did not make much difference to Babur; he turned back from the march on Delhi, trounced the Khan completely, and carried on. Characteristically, Babur's attitude was sufficiently lighthearted and relaxed to enable him to visit a particularly pretty fountain and take a river trip with drinking companions even after he came within sight of the Delhi army. And it was a massive force: Ibrahim is said to have brought out 100,000 men and nearly 100 elephants. Babur had 12,000 men. Not surprisingly, his forces felt a little daunted by the thought of the immense opposition; but for a week the two armies faced each other, while Babur's men entrenched themselves firmly and recovered their nerve. In no degree could Ibrahim match Babur as a commander, and in the Delhi army there was much disaffection and little discipline. The result was a rout. The Turks and Mongols employed their usual tactics of surrounding the enemy with swift, light detachments; the Indians followed their tradition and advanced *en masse*. The smaller force simply ran rings around the larger, rings which drew tighter and tighter until the Indians were so squashed together that they could not use their strength at all. Afterwards Babur wrote:

> The sun had mounted spear-high when the onset began, and the battle lasted till midday, when the enemy were completely broken and routed, and my people victorious and triumphant. By the grace and mercy of Almighty God this difficult affair was made easy for me, and that mighty army, in the space of half a day, was laid in the dust.

The spoil was enormous. Humayun, Babur's son, literally made his fortune that day. All the chief barons received enough to keep themselves in comfort for years; every soldier received his share, and so did all the camp followers. Even the people back in Kabul were sent gold and silver, cloth, jewels and slaves. The royal treasuries at Delhi and Agra yielded fabulous quantities of precious stuff; and Humayun, who had advanced to occupy Agra in his father's name, found one very particular jewel.

The governor of Agra, Raja Bikramajit of Gwalior, had fought and died with Ibrahim Lodi. His family crouched, terrified for their lives, in the fort of Agra; they had good reason to be frightened, for the Mongol troops were sacking the city around them. But when Humayun arrived, he followed the example frequently given by Babur and ordered the looting to stop. He also assured the royal family of his personal protection, and they reciprocated with the presentation of a huge diamond, which, Babur recorded, 'is said to be worth half the daily expenditure of the whole world'. Humayun in turn presented the jewel to Babur as a tribute; and Babur, whose loves were simply nature and empire, promptly gave it back.

And with Humayun it stayed – for the time being. For the first time a diamond that is not legend or myth, symbol or fantasy, enters the story – a truly historical stone of 186 carats in weight. The Koh-i-noor, when it arrived in England, weighed 186 carats. This correspondence of weights seems to go far beyond chance or coincidence, and the gem known as 'Babur's diamond' – though he never really possessed it at all – has often been identified with cheerful confidence as the original Koh-i-noor. But as will be seen in due course, the question of its identity is not quite so simple.

Babur, meanwhile, did not think much of India. Its sole advantages, so far as he could tell, were that it was a large country with masses of gold and silver, and that it could provide a lot of cheap, skilled labour. Against this, however, there were myriad disadvantages: heat, dust, bad architecture, unfriendly, rude and stupid people, 'no horses, no good flesh, no grapes or musk-melons, no good fruits, no ice or cold water, no good food or bread in the bazaars, no baths or colleges, no candles, no torches, not even a candlestick'. And above all – no gardens.

Babur decided to make his capital at Agra. It was, at any rate, well watered by the Jumna, and one of the first things he did was to order the laying-out of a garden. The site he chose was across the river from the town, and he did not really like it; but soon the ground was cleared, and the typical accoutrements of a Persian garden began to appear: a well, a tank, a pavilion, a bath-house.

> There in that charmless and disorderly Hind, plots of gardens were laid out with order and symmetry, with suitable borders and parterres in every corner, and in every border rose and narcissus in perfect arrangement.

At first the Indians had assumed that Babur, like most previous conquerors, would simply sack their cities and go away, but when they realized he intended to stay, they began to assess him more carefully; and, on the whole, they liked what they saw. If he was sometimes severe, he was far more frequently magnanimous and generous, and he was certainly a great improvement on the despotic Ibrahim Lodi; so gradually more and more people came to offer allegiance to him. Perhaps the tribute that touched him most was the name they gave to his wonderful garden, the like of which they had never seen – they called it Kabul. Certainly he was sometimes very homesick for his adopted country; one day one of the delightful musk-melons of Kabul was brought to him. 'As I cut it up, I felt a deep homesickness and a sense of exile from my native land, and I could not help shedding tears,' he wrote. The evocative taste and smell touched him deeply, and he determined to have a highway built, 900 miles long, to run from Agra to Kabul.

Many paintings exist of Babur: in battles, in hunts, in ceremonies and celebrations. One shows him transferred from his garden in Kabul to the one nostalgically named Kabul, beside Agra. He sits on a dais of cushions beneath an ornamented canopy, receiving ambassadors from the Uzbeg and Rajput clans. He is surrounded once again by blossoming shrubs, flowers and fruit trees; birds alight once again on the branches beside him. The ambassadors bow respectfully; attendants fan the king; and with a watchful but calm expression, he inclines his head to the foreigners. Behind him runs the Jumna, and beyond its banks rise the walls and towers of Agra.

Babur did not live long enough to make a lasting individual impression on India; his death came in 1530, only four years after the conquest of Delhi; but the wedge he drove continued to probe deeply into the tree of Indian society. And though at first it produced rivalry, jealousy and hatred – an open split between conquerors and conquered – at length the wedge was driven so deep that it became a part of the tree, and the wound closed behind it. The classical Indian time-sense, the sense of cyclical rather than linear time, produces a sense of living in a perpetual present around which past and future revolve, equidistant and equally unimportant. A situation of constant flux, a constant balancing of forces, has as a natural corollary the feeling that each moment is a crisis, and from any point of view the advent of the Moguls was a crisis for India. But crisis has two positive aspects: the lesser is that retrospectively it often seems to have been natural and inevitable; the greater is that it is dynamic. And a very important point in understanding the Indian idea of unity is to remember that unity does not mean uniformity – rather it is an interrelation of differences, an organic concept in which root, cell, sap, leaf and branch together form the tree. The process of assimilation was slow, but from its first painful, unwelcome thrusts, the Mogul energy percolated through India in twin streams of reaction and co-operation, both of which were creative. The result was one of the greatest organisms seen in the subcontinent: the flowering of Mogul India.

Humayun, Babur's son, was a king with fortunes as variable as those of his father. He has been aptly called 'Humayun the hyphen', linking the first Mogul inroads to India with their subsequent consolidation under his son Akbar. Technically he reigned for twenty-four years, from 1526 to 1550, but much of his time was spent in exile while more able opposing generals of the *ancien régime* reclaimed the rule of Babur's territories. However, two items of particular interest emerged from his life and death: first, the fate of his celebrated jewel, won after the fall of Agra; and secondly, his tomb.

The various vicissitudes of Humayun's reign led him in 1543 to Persia, where he requested asylum with the shah. They met in 1544; and for the shah it was a triumph, albeit unexpected, to have the nominal Emperor of India as a guest at his court, and Humayun was fêted. Nevertheless he was very much in the role of paying guest; to be a refugee was bad enough, but to be a sponge would have been much worse. He was able to salve some of the sense of dishonour by presenting the shah with a large quantity of jewels, among which was the diamond. *En route* to Persia, the more lowly Indian rulers with whom he had tarried had tried to acquire the jewel, but Humayun had guarded it jealously. On one occasion a courtier posing as a diamond merchant had tried to buy it, and Humayun had had him thrown out of the camp with a comment that was to become famous – 'Such jewels', he said, 'cannot be bought. Either they are won in battle, or they are passed on as an honourable gift.' Certainly it was passed on to the shah, and certainly it was a very honourable gift. Less certain is the assertion that from the Shah of Persia it was returned to India. Having won the diamond easily, the shah, it is said, let it go easily; one tradition claims that, as head of the Shiite sect of Islam, he presented it a few years later to the ruler of the Deccan, who was also a Shiite. This tradition was snapped up eagerly by some historians. We shall leave it for the moment, however, and investigate it in the next chapter, where the question of identity becomes especially important.

Humayun tripped through his reign with an air of dilettante irresponsibility, sometimes conducting a brilliant campaign and winning great territories, sometimes losing them again after relaxing for a year or so and ignoring his rivals. In the same way he tripped out of life: browsing in his library one day he heard the call to prayers, and realizing that he was late he ran out, fell down the steps of the library, and found his final excuse for shedding earthly responsibility.

A casual visitor to his tomb might well be excused for thinking he had come to a palace by accident. It is an immense structure of red sandstone and white marble, set on a large platform of red sandstone; the lowest level is surrounded by graceful pointed Persian arches, the next with similar, larger arches, some setting deeply into the whole construction, some more shallow, all decorated with six-pointed stars and the delicate interlacing of the arabesque. Above the upper arches rise small, fine pillars and the very Indian *chhatris*, little pavilions ornamenting the roof; and above them all stands the great dome. It is a double dome: its outer layer corresponds to the proportions of the exterior, its inner layer to the interior, so that harmony is preserved within and without. It was the first double dome built in India, and it owed its existence to Persian architecture; it is one of the best-proportioned domes in all India. It lies south-east of Delhi, its shining white marble making it stand out from all the rest of the landscape.

Despite the *chhatris*, the whole thing is unmistakably Persian and Islamic; and therein lies one of its most important aspects. Babur, for all his gardens and conquests, had never been a builder of any great degree; he never stayed in one place for long enough. But Humayun's tomb marks the beginning of a series of magnificent funereal architecture. Indeed, though there had been a good deal of Indo-Islamic architecture even before Babur's conquest, Humayun's tomb could justifiably be seen as the first major step towards the fusion of Indian and Islamic building. At first, two architectural styles of greater difference could hardly be imagined; Persian architecture, essentially a study of space and line, came into contact with an architecture of mass. Their wedding produced something romantic, a little more solemn and with a graceful touch of sadness. The union was inevitable, for though the Moslems imported foreign ideas such as the minaret, the dome and the pointed arch, they had to rely on local labour to realize their visions, and local labour interpreted the new ideas in terms of their own cultural heritage. And then, under Humayun's son Akbar, the Indo-Persian organism began to flourish fully.

Akbar means 'Great', and the first thing to be said about the Emperor Akbar is that he lived up to his name. He was one of the greatest rulers India has ever had, and was certainly the greatest since Mauryan times. Like Asoka, his empire came to include almost the whole of India, and like Asoka, his rule had an important religious aspect – entirely appropriate in a land where politics and religion are frequently indistinguishable. But the comparison with Asoka should not be taken too far – for one thing, Asoka was a native king; Akbar inherited a Mogul throne that was almost as tenuous as it had been under the first conquests of his grandfather Babur. At his coronation he was three months short of his fourteenth birthday, another boy-king; by his death he was emperor of a vast heterogeneous realm, incorporating several different social, cultural and religious traditions into a relatively harmonious whole. With a kingdom that was unified but not uniform, he might well be called the king of organic unity.

It seems quite likely that the key point of integration between alien cultures, the point where conquerors and conquered begin to come together irrevocably to form a new culture, is when they begin to fall in love with one another. Marriages of political convenience have been a commonplace event in many periods, with or without love, and one of Akbar's early moves towards union was to marry a Rajput princess. To have a Hindu wife, a member of the aristocratic martial clans, was at the least an astute political move; the heir to the throne was half Rajput, and automatically the Hindu attitude began to change. Apart from its intrinsic value, the marriage represented the last of the four areas of Akbar's particular genius, which together made Mogul rule an accepted fact of Hindu life, a source of national pride rather than a barely tolerated conquest. Though it is clearly a simplification, the four areas can be seen as expansion, union, consolidation and – perhaps most importantly – imagination. Any imperial ruler, or any ruler with imperial pretensions, has the first three qualities, or strives for them; but the fourth, the power of creative imagination, is the one which distinguishes the imperial genius from the ordinary emperor. Aggressive expansion was a basic tenet of Akbar's policies; throughout his reign he conducted campaigns of invasion and subjugation, which extended the empire, finally, throughout the northern half of India, from Kabul to Gujarat to Bengal. It was really only his son's simmering state of near-insurrection, in Akbar's later years, that restricted his movements towards the south.

In a sense it could be said that Akbar invented India. Apart from welding together its diverse political and religious traditions, and extending and consolidating its boundaries, he also established an efficient administrative structure that lasted, essentially unchanged, until the end of the Mogul empire in the mid nineteenth century, and which to some extent was inherited by the British Raj. The administration was not his original creation, however; it was owed to Sher Shah, the Afghan who had reconquered large areas of Babur's India. Two of the most notable aspects of the system were a fairness of taxes on crops, whereby a crop which failed could not be taxed, and a close supervision of viceroys and fief-holders, in order that none should begin to have pretensions of independence. This latter element was eventually extended to the point where fief-holders were compelled to live in court, while their fiefs were run by employees. Every fief-holder had to provide a certain number of horses and men for military service, and in earlier days they had often borrowed troops from one another to make up numbers for inspection. Akbar stopped this by instituting a branding system; the horses could not be duplicated, and as men and horses went together, it provided an effective check. He also began a carefully graded series of military ranks, in which men and officers were paid in cash rather than by the tributes they could exact from a province. Not surprisingly, none of these innovations was very popular, and their establishment was a slow affair; but once they were established, they were so manifestly based on justice that the ordinary people began to decide that having a Mogul emperor was probably to their advantage.

Popular loyalty was also increased by Akbar's abolition of the *jizya*, a tax on non-Moslems; having a Mogul emperor was most certainly advantageous. The decision was strengthened even more when the emperor had a son; the boy's mother was the Rajput princess, which went a long way to salving the Hindu sense of honour. The boy, named Salim, was born in a place called Sikri, about twenty-six miles west of Agra. The birth took place there because a particular saint, after whom the boy was named, had prophesied that an heir was due, and the saint's cell was at Sikri. A little while later there was a lot more: Akbar built a new capital there and called it Fathepur Sikri – the Victory City of Sikri.

Fathepur Sikri, more than any other of his creations, epitomizes the dream of Akbar's reign. Light, airy and open, it has at its heart an enormous throne set high on a pillar. Here the emperor would sit and give audience, the turning-point of the world. And an audience was granted to everybody – one of Akbar's most important characteristics was that he would listen to opinions, arguments, complaints and requests from any one of his subjects. But the final decision on any matter always rested with him. This was the key to his power: he simultaneously set himself apart from all his people, so that no one group dominated another, and yet all had equally free access to him. Fathepur Sikri was a glorious mushroom growth of terraces and courtyards, mosques, tombs and palaces, all constructed in nine years – a region of wild hills and deserts transformed into a magnificent city. Its builders were drawn from every part of the empire, and their architectural idiosyncrasies show through; but the style of the whole was united by the emperor's personal taste, in which the cultural sensitivity of the Persian was allied with the energy of the Turk and the Turkish knack of grasping the essentials of an alien civilization. Outside the tomb of the saint, Salim, twisting serpentine brackets curl up from walls to eaves – very Hindu. Equally Hindu are the four-pillared *chhatris* which punctuate the skyline, and the massive ornamentation on the house of a Brahman, Raja Birbal, who – typically – was one of Akbar's closest associates. In fact there is only one building in the entire complex which is unequivocally Moslem, and that is the great mosque, the Jama Masjid, which dominates the city.

The relation between politics and religion, always close in India, was made absolute. Akbar had always been sympathetic to religions other than Islam, believing that all sprang from a common truth, though they expressed it differently. While he was an orthodox Moslem, he frequently disagreed with the *ulema*, the Moslem priesthood, and equally frequently found himself hampered by their pronouncements, which controlled a large part of the lives of many of his subjects. Moreover, there was the fact of his marriages to Hindu princesses; Sunnite Moslems did not recognize the marriages as legal, since Akbar had more than four wives, and though the Shiites recognized them, it was only as 'temporary' marriages. Accepting the former view would jeopardize relations with the Rajputs; accepting the latter, with the implication that he was becoming Shiite, would alienate the majority of the army chieftains. Akbar's answer to the problems was to create a new religion.

About fifty years after Henry VIII proclaimed himself head of church and state in England, Akbar did a similar thing in India. The new religion was called the Din-i-Illahi, the Divine Faith; it was an eclectic faith, combining aspects of Islam, Hinduism and Christianity with a heavy flavour of Zoroastrianism, and it placed the emperor in a semi-divine status, the temporal representative of the godhead. Loyalty to the emperor became a matter above politics; treason became sacrilege.

However, the move was not purely coldly political; it sprang from a series of debates organized by the emperor between the various sects of Islam and the other religions, debates which were supposed to expose charlatans and reveal truth. The motive appears to have been a genuine religious curiosity on Akbar's part, and his solution was not simply an outburst of annoyance and frustration against the quarrelling theologians. He had an extremely strong personal experience of enlightenment, which convinced him that a direct communion with God was possible.

He announced his new faith in a dramatically symbolic manner. The *khutba*, the hymn of praise to Allah, was traditionally read in the name of the emperor. One day Akbar himself climbed into the priest's position and read the *khutba*, ending it as usual with the words *Allah Akbar* – 'God is Great'. But the same words could mean 'Akbar is God'.

Whether or not he hoped that his faith would spread is uncertain. In fact, it was never practised by more than a small group of his closest courtiers, and it faded away after his death. But during his life it did have the highly important effect of placing him in a position where all people could feel loyal to and supported by the emperor. He had contrived to remove himself from the highly charged emotional arenas of religion and politics while remaining in control of both.

Akbar's life had been a masterly balancing of opposing, or at least diverse, forces, often conducted directly in the battlefield with the sword, or more subtly with words and persuasion. His death at least was a peaceful affair, and, for a man of his extraordinary stature, rather pathetically banal. He caught dysentery. The remedies offered only made him worse, and at the age of sixty-three, having ruled for forty-nine years, he died.

In many ways his reign was the zenith of the Mogul Empire. The uniform administration he had imposed on the country was so efficient that his heirs had only to continue with it; he had accumulated so much wealth that even without further income they could have continued to live in the same fabulously ostentatious style; he had made erstwhile revolutionary kingdoms and principalities into loyal provinces; he had created an atmosphere of extraordinary tolerance between many different traditions of culture and religion; and had gone beyond that to initiate a genuine cultural synthesis between two very different ways of life.

The fate of Fathepur Sikri was curious. Salim, Akbar's eldest son, born at Sikri, inherited the crown at the age of thirty-six – not before time, in his opinion. That was in the year 1605; the last time that Akbar had been to his City of Victory had been twenty years before. The city which had taken nine years to build was used as the capital for less than five years more. The site turned out to be miasmic and unhealthy, and in 1585 Fathepur Sikri was abandoned. It has remained deserted ever since, a unique epitaph to one of the most truly universal of India's emperors.

From Babur and Humayun, the first possessors of an indisputably historical diamond, we have taken this digression through the life of Akbar because – though he had no direct contact with such a jewel – it is impossible to ignore him. Not only did his reign realize the dream of the *chakravartin* in one vast, tolerant, efficient and heterogeneous empire, but he set up the solid, practical blueprint of a popular rule that was to continue relatively undisturbed for more than 200 years. The solidity of his pattern of monarchy is demonstrated by its continuance, quite unchanged, through the twenty-three years of the reign of his incompetent son Salim. Of Salim, little need be said; on ascending to the throne he took the name of Jahangir – 'World-Grasper' – and the avaricious pretentiousness of the title turned out to be a fairly accurate vignette of his personality. Despite a high intelligence, he was content to let others do the practical work of ruling in his name; he preferred to spend his time with his women, his opium, his wine, poetry and paintings. Possessed of immeasurable wealth, the fortunate hedonist was able to extend the cultural life of his court without having to bother much about his empire. So, passing the 'World-Grasper' with a nod of acknowledgement, we shall go straight to his son and grandson, Shah Jahan and Aurangzeb; and with them we shall find the diamond.

> The desire of seeing the world, which had induced me to visit Palestine and Egypt, still prompted me to extend my travels, and I formed the design of exploring the Red Sea from one end to the other. In pursuance of this plan, I quitted Grand Cairo, where I had resided more than a year, and in two-and-thirty hours (travelling at a Caravan-rate) reached the town of Suez. Here I embarked in a galley and was conveyed in seventeen days, always hugging the coast, to Gidda. Further sailing along the shores of Arabia Felix brought me in fifteen days to Moka; thence I embarked in an Indian vessel, and in twenty-two days arrived at Surat, in Hindustan, the empire of the Great Mogul. I found that the reigning prince was named Shah Jahan or King of the World.

François Bernier arrived in India in 1658. It was a time of dire crisis for the Mogul Empire; Shah Jahan was old and very ill, and his four sons had forced the empire into a long and bloody civil war of succession. Bernier, skilled in medicine, found employment in the royal court, and from his unusual position was able to observe all the traumatic events of the period. He recorded all he saw with great accuracy and attention to detail; he had a cynical, scientific eye without any romantic illusions about the human motives in the actions he witnessed. But he also had a sense of humour, and a sense of the absurd, and these qualities combined with his scrupulous precision to give his records great clarity and an air of real humanity.

By 1658, Shah Jahan had been emperor for thirty years; the dynasty founded by Babur had been growing for 132 years, and was in full flower. After Babur the gardener, Shah Jahan was the builder; it was he who created that most famous of all Indian buildings, the Taj Mahal. By comparison with Fathepur Sikri, or with Akbar's tomb at Sikandra, the Taj Mahal is strikingly Persian in style; the synthesis of Akbar's architecture had faded before a revival of ancestral modes of building, and yet by a strange paradox the Taj Mahal is almost always acclaimed as the highest and purest point of Mogul architecture.

> The columns, the architraves and the cornices are indeed not formed according to the five properties of architecture so strictly observed in French edifices. The building is of a different and peculiar kind, but not without something pleasing in its whimsical structure.

Bernier began his description of the tomb very cautiously; he feared that his taste might have become 'corrupted' from living so long in India, and because he admired the Taj Mahal intensely, he wanted to share his admiration with others. The trouble was that the Taj Mahal was definitely not French, and it could be a hard task to convince the conservative Gallic disposition that there was anything worthwhile outside France.

> It consists almost wholly of arches upon arches, and galleries upon galleries, disposed and contrived in a hundred different ways. *Nevertheless* the edifice has a magnificent appearance, and is conceived and executed effectually. Nothing offends the eye; on the contrary, it is delighted with every part, and never tired with looking.

He was considerably relieved when a fellow Frenchman, visiting the tomb with him, said that 'he had seen nothing in Europe so bold and majestic'. In fact, the second opinion was from a man as pro-Indian as Bernier, a jeweller named Tavernier, a man who was to play a key part in the tale of the Koh-i-noor; but the Taj Mahal became as renowned as Bernier had hoped.

Three years before Bernier's arrival in India, on 17 December 1655, a Persian named Mir Jumla was present at the court of Shah Jahan. The emperor was staggering through the final crisis of his reign; he had been ill for so long that, while he was still very much alive, his sons were already battling for supremacy. Mir Jumla had taken sides with Aurangzeb, the third son; previously he had been wazir to the King of Golkonda, but he had been caught *in flagrante delicto* with the king's mother, and had to leave Golkonda in a rather precipitate manner. He was immensely rich and a very able general, and so when he threw himself on the mercy of the Mogul he was welcomed with open arms. He persuaded the Mogul to go to war against the King of Golkonda, pointing out the wealth of the country and reiterating once more the old notion of extending the empire from coast to coast; and 'on this occasion it was that he presented Shah Jahan with that celebrated diamond which has generally been deemed unparalleled in size and beauty'. The stone had no name, or at least none is recorded, but it came to be known as the 'Great Mogul'. It was extremely large – in Indian terms its weight was 900 *ratis*, equivalent to $787\frac{1}{2}$ Florentine carats. Between Babur's diamond and the new stone, there was no comparison.

Two

The Merchant-Traveller

Tavernier and the Emperor Aurangzeb – early European contacts with India – the port of Goa – Indian methods of diamond mining – Tavernier and Mir Jumla – Tavernier sees the 'Great Mogul' – Babur's diamond, the Great Mogul and the Koh-i-noor – the Peacock Throne – Tavernier's mysterious death

On the first day of November 1665, a European visitor to the court of Aurangzeb requested a last audience with the Great Mogul. The visitor, a Frenchman, was a stout man, heavily built and not particularly tall. From the caravanserai where he and his followers lodged, he went alone in his coach through the pungent, colourful streets of Shahjahanabad. The new capital of the Mogul Empire lay side by side with Old Delhi; eventually the two would merge and be seen as one, but at that time they were distinct. The old city was ruinous, a web of narrow streets and bamboo shacks. Only three or four nobles of the court lived there, their tents pitched in large private gardens. The rest was a habitation for the poor, and for priests.

The building of Shahjahanabad, the new city, had commenced less than thirty years before. It was a great straggling town of merchants and courtiers. Its main street was a long, wide bazaar coming through from the old side and leading to the central square, where the imperial palace lay. Each side of the bazaar was lined with arches, and under every arch stood a merchant among his goods. The two oxen pulling the Frenchman's little coach made a slow passage through the crowds, whose shouts and cries came to him through the coach's open window, mingling, in the hot dry air, with smells of dust and spices.

The man's name was Jean-Baptiste Tavernier. From the portraits that remain of him, a chubby, serious face looks out, a double chin and heavy cheeks framing a long and slightly hooked nose. The eyes are heavily lidded, too; but through the air of weighty seriousness, they have a wry look, and on the mouth there is the faint beginning of a smile. In a lifetime of travelling he had seen things which were mere fables to his countrymen – elephants and fakirs, Moslems and Hindus, Mogul tombs and palaces – and he had seen them so often that in his old age he could afford an indulgent air.

Tavernier, by inclination, was a traveller, and by profession a diamond-merchant. On that November morning, trundling along to take his leave of the Great Mogul, he was in his sixtieth year, and almost half-way through his final journey around Asia. He had made five previously, going as far south as Madras and as far east as Dacca; together, the six journeys lasted twenty-four years. He went rarely by sea; the overland routes were covered on horseback, or, more usually, in ox-drawn carts and carriages. For his final journey, he had a coach made for him, in the Parisian style. He was very proud of it – not only did it have curtains and cushions, it had suspension as well. Drawn by a very expensive pair of trotting bullocks, he could cover thirty-five miles in a day, followed by a troop of servants, porters and companions – a group that could number anything from ten to 100 or more.

But though Tavernier was one of the greatest travellers of his age, he was by no means the first European to see India. Contact had existed between the continent and the sub-continent since the days of Alexander; Indian ambassadors had been sent to Rome, along with merchants, prostitutes, ascetics, and many other exotic people and products. Roman soldiers had come to India to serve as mercenaries; and, more importantly, Roman gold had come as well. India, exporting her spices, jewels, iron and animals, had little need of the goods that Europe could offer, and received payment almost entirely in gold and silver. Wine and horses contributed a small part to the balance of trade, but from the time of Nero onwards, the flow of gold to India formed a very real and serious factor in Roman finance. Centuries later, English mercantilists complained of the 'Indian silver drain' in much the same way.

After the fall of Rome, trade had continued, and indeed flourished, mostly by overland routes with Moslem Arabs acting as middlemen, towards the end of the Middle Ages – the later fifteenth and early sixteenth centuries. The twin threats of Turkish and Mongol invasions on land, and near-monopoly by Venice and Egypt on the sea, had prompted the first commercial voyages of the Portuguese. Vasco da Gama made landfall on the western Indian coast in 1498, a century and a half before Tavernier's time. In the period between the two travellers, the Portuguese Eastern empire rose and fell, and the Dutch and English established firm commercial networks. The failure of the former, and the lasting effect of the latter two, was, ironically, owed to the very wish of the Portuguese to influence India. Da Gama and his men, coming from the Catholic Renaissance, sailed in an atmosphere very like that of the Crusades; in da Gama's famous phrase, they were looking for 'Christians and spices'. Their descendants were similarly imbued with the spirit of the Counter-Reformation, a precise, dogmatic and intolerant view of religion and life which met its match in the comparable attitudes of the Moslems. India was well used to the frontal onslaught of different religions.

The Dutch and English, by contrast, came for purely commercial reasons, and since this was comparatively beneficial to all, the mutual influence, in terms of respect, understanding and profit, was far greater. However, da Gama's achievement should not be underrated; there was a Portuguese presence in India for a century before the first Dutch fleet sailed there, and in that century some lasting legacies were made to Indian life. One of the most notable of these was the port of Goa, half-way down the western coast. This became the capital of the Portuguese Eastern empire; Tavernier visited it in 1641 and again in 1648.

The city had been captured by the Portuguese in 1510 from the Sultan of Bijapur, and though their control of the Indian Ocean had begun to fade from 1622, Tavernier still described Goa as one of the three finest ports in Europe and Asia. The other two were Constantinople and – patriotically – Toulon. There is a touch of homesickness in his account of Goa: 'the island abounds in corn and rice, and produces numerous fruits, as mangoes, pineapples, plantains and coconuts; but a good pippin is certainly worth more than all these fruits'. Goa, none the less, could afford other pleasures. Tavernier found on his second visit that many of the rich families had fallen on hard times, and it often happened that one or other of the ladies, 'without abating anything of their pride', would come to ask alms of him – always late at night. 'I was *honour bound* to invite her in to partake of refreshment,' he protests, 'which would sometimes last till the following day.'

Goa, in fact, was famous for its women, and as famous for the jealousy of their husbands, who were singularly fond of killing their wives, either by poison or the knife, at the least suggestion of infidelity. One hopes Tavernier was discreet.

There were other more usual reasons for the fame of Goa. It was, at least by repute, a great centre of health, both physical and spiritual. The hospital there was known throughout India for the high proportion of cures effected by its doctors – a surprisingly high proportion, considering that the two main methods of treatment were bleeding the patient, and then administering cow's urine as a medicinal drink. The spiritual needs of the city were provided for on two fronts: apart from the archbishop and his clergy, there were six different orders of

THE MOGUL'S DIAMOND
(of Tavernier).

NAMED *Koh-i-nur* BY NÁDIR SHÁH IN 1739.

Figures illustrating its mutilated condition when brought to England in 1850.

FIG. I. The circle is of the same diameter as the Mogul's Diamond, figured by Tavernier (see Book II, chap. xxii, Plate II). The shaded portion represents the basal surface of the *Koh-i-nur*.

FIG. II. The *Koh-i-nur*, showing the surfaces from whence portions had been removed by cleavage. A, Flaw parallel to cleavage plane H; B and C, Notches cut to hold the stone in its setting; D, Flaw parallel to plane G, produced by fracture at E; F, Fracture produced by a blow; G, Unpolished cleavage plane produced by fracture—it was inclined at an angle of 109° 28' to the basal plane H. From Mr. Tennant's figure.

FIG. III. The opposite aspect of the *Koh-i-nur* from a glass model.

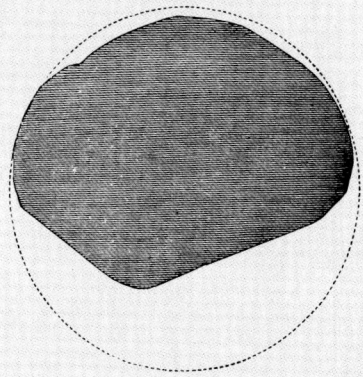

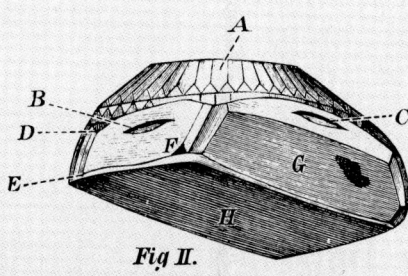

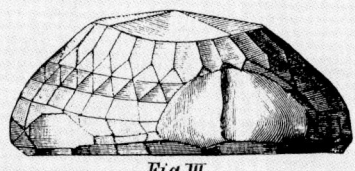

above:

The Koh-i-noor identified as Tavernier's Mogul's Diamond from Valentine Ball's translation of his *Six Voyages*

left:

Jean-Baptiste Tavernier in 1679, at the height of his success, dressed in robes of honour

top left:

The Emperor Jahangir (1605-27), the 'World-Grasper', receiving Prince Parviz in audience

left:

Detail from an unfinished portrait of Aurangzeb

top right:

The second version of the Peacock Throne. The throne described by Tavernier was broken up and reconstructed to this design

above:

The fruits of India: a magnificent cabinet in ivory and rosewood from seventeenth-century Goa made for the Portuguese market

opposite:

A Mogul painting, *c*.1600, of a European receiving a message while his servants prepare refreshments

A drunken feast from the Hamzah Nameh, 1564-79

monks – Dominicans, Augustins, Cordeliers, Barefoot Carmelites, Jesuits and Capuchins; and for those who were not as spiritually ordered as they should be, there was the Inquisition. Tavernier met the Inquisitor, who, having enjoyed the traveller's stories, invited him to dinner at a mansion belonging to the Barefoot Carmelites. It was, Tavernier noted, one of the most beautiful buildings in India – a splendid palace, given to the monks by a nobleman who had died of leprosy; but he made no comment on the Inquisitor.

The simplest reason for Goa's fame, though, was its wealth. In its hey-day the Viceroyalty of Goa was one of the most lucrative posts it was possible to hold in the whole world. Subordinate to the viceroyalty were five seats of local government, which in themselves were richer than most ordinary viceroyalties. The most important of these was Mozambique; there was a healthy trade there in ivory and ambergris, and one governor came away at the end of his three years in office with ambergris worth 200,000 *ecus*, or about £450,000. It was quite usual for a governor to make a profit of 500,000 crowns or so – roughly a million pounds – in the three years allotted him. Another governor thought the system so good that he proposed extending the term of office to eight years.

Sea trade occupied a far greater proportion of the market than trade overland: one calculation puts the annual weight of seaborne goods then as 60,000 tons, compared with only 500 tons a year passing overland. But diamonds were light in weight and very profitable, and Tavernier, on the whole, preferred land travel. Though he did go by sea sometimes, he was too often involved with storms and leaky ships to feel happy about it. One such instance came shortly after his departure from Goa. He had decided to sail to Bantam in western Java, and the voyage did not begin well; the captain of the ship had never sailed on the Indian coasts before, and could not read the weather. A terrible storm blew up, so violent and prolonged that the rudder was broken and all seven anchors were lost. Matters were not helped by the fact that most of the people on board, including Tavernier, were suffering from very bad hangovers. Two days before the storm they had all drunk a great deal of local palm wine, which was far stronger than expected; so by midnight on the night of the storm everyone had begun to 'examine his conscience' and they all prayed. And it certainly seemed to work: at the very last moment, with the ship about to be driven on to rocks, the wind suddenly changed direction and they were blown off to safety.

The lure of diamonds was so strong for Tavernier that he was quite willing, on many occasions, to travel through country that other merchants, and even Indians, would do their best to avoid. He never really felt at home on sea, least of all along the Malabar coast, which was infested with pirates; but on land the prospect of encountering bandits or tigers never seemed to deter him at all. Once, travelling with eight servants and sixty foot-soldiers, he arrived at the territory of the Raja of Bargant. The soldiers promptly stopped and refused to go any further; the raja, they said, lived entirely by robbery, and without a doubt their entire company – Tavernier and his servants included – would be waylaid and strangled if they dared to cross the area. The merchant argued with them for a long time, accusing them of cowardice. They freely admitted it. Making a quick tour of the neighbouring villages, Tavernier engaged a further fifty men, and prepared once more to enter Bargant, now escorted by 110 soldiers altogether; but the same thing happened again. The fifty newcomers, realizing the route they were to take, changed their minds about going. For the three days' work involved, Tavernier offered them the normal wage for a month, but he could not persuade them. The soldiers' attitude frightened his own servants so much that three of them became faint-hearted as well, and eventually Tavernier set off with only his two coachmen and the remaining servants for company.

He had gone five miles when he saw a group of fifty armed horsemen ahead. The merchant distributed arms to his five companions, and they put themselves in a posture of defence; then, as the first group of the riders approached, Tavernier was recognized by one of them. It was a lieutenant to whom he had given brandy and wine on an earlier journey through Bargant. The meeting was fortunate; the raja himself arrived, and since Tavernier quickly gave him tobacco and wine, a party ensued which lasted two days, with drinking, hunting and dancing-girls in attendance. At the end of it all, Tavernier, far from being strangled, was escorted through Bargant by 200 of the raja's own horsemen, and was warmly invited to return.

Further rumours of perilous rivers and wild beasts failed to prevent him from visiting four of the mines where diamonds were found. It was extremely rare that a European merchant should actually venture to the mines themselves; Tavernier, indeed, firmly believed that he was the first to do so. In fact, at least three Europeans had preceded him, when a traveller called William Methold led a group to the mine of Kollur in 1622.

Kollur was situated close to the river Krishna, in the state of Andra Pradesh. The river there makes a large loop around a mountain range, and the mine lay on the plain between the mountains and the river. When Tavernier visited it in 1653, there were 60,000 people working there, men, women and children. All the work was open-cast; none of the pits Tavernier saw was more than fourteen foot deep, because digging would cease when the miners reached water. He was very surprised by the methods of mining: almost as much attention was paid to ceremonies beforehand as to the actual digging. Prayers would be offered by a priest for protection from the evil spirits of the mine, with the employer and all the miners – fifty or 100 to a pit – prostrating themselves before a statue of one of the gods. The priest would anoint the forehead of each worker with the *tilak*, the sectarial mark made of saffron and gum, and then, after washing their bodies, all would eat a meal of rice and butter.

The first stage of mining was to build an enclosure, two feet high, of the same circumference as the mine itself. All the earth dug out would be put in this enclosure and sluiced with water for two or three days, after which it would be sieved, beaten with large wooden pestles and sieved again. Finally, the miners would search by hand through the sand that was left to extract the precious stones. It was simple but effective, and the method contained at least one improvement on earlier times – previously, the earth would be beaten not with wood, but with rocks, and that, Tavernier lamented, produced many flaws in the diamonds.

Around the site of the mine were scattered a large number of diamond-cutters. These men were of particular interest to Tavernier, since he knew something of the art of cutting. In contrast to the European approach, in which a stone would be worked in such a way that the maximum brilliance and play of light was obtained, the Indian ideal was to maintain the stone's size as far as possible. The cutter would scarcely touch a good clean stone; facets would be put on only to conceal small flaws or spots within a gem. Knowing this, Tavernier quickly learnt to detect flaws; and unfortunately many of the diamonds were fractured by the miners. A diamond was supposed to be so strong it would withstand any blow, and to the merchant's horror, he learned that an archaic method of testing a diamond's quality was to beat it on an anvil with a hammer. The theory was that a true diamond would shatter the hammer, but though diamonds are extremely hard, they are very brittle. No one knows how many gems were destroyed in this way. Many diamonds were damaged in the mining process as well, especially at the mine of Rammalakota, where a method different from that of Kollur was used. At Rammalakota, the diamonds were found in sandy veins in rocks. To extract them the miners used iron probes and crowbars, often harming the jewels with their over-zealous blows.

European cutters used iron wheels for working their gems; the Indians used steel. Tavernier admired the skill of the Indian cutters, but deplored the steel wheels; they had to be removed from their stands every twenty-four hours to be reground, and since the cutter was generally unable to replace the wheel exactly as it had been before, a single stone could not be worked in a consistent way. Iron wheels only needed filing to sharpen them, and this could be done on the stand.

Kollur was an important mine for several reasons. Not only was it one of the largest mines, but it also produced some of the largest stones, though their water was not usually clear. Mir Jumla, during his time in the service of the King of Golkonda, had had overall responsibility for many diamond mines, and Kollur was one of them. Few of the mines were actually farmed under his name; he acquired their leases from the king under several different aliases. But all the ones that he controlled were farmed extremely efficiently, and their proceeds were one of the bases of his immense wealth. Bernier commented that 'people spoke of nothing but the riches of Mir Jumla, and of the plenty of his diamonds, which were not reckoned but by sacks'. How many sacks of his gems came from Kollur is anyone's guess; but one stone in particular certainly came from there, and that was the one that he presented to Shah Jahan.

Tavernier met Mir Jumla on several occasions, and had a healthy respect for him, both as one of the most powerful men in India and as an astute fellow-businessman. The first time they met was in 1652, when Mir Jumla was Grand Wazir, or prime minister, to the king of Golkonda. Tavernier was carrying a quantity of large pearls that he wished to sell to the king, and by custom had to show them to the wazir first; only goods that met with his approval could go through to the king himself. Tavernier was impressed by the promptness and firmness of Mir Jumla's responses to every request made of him; and since their meeting took place only eight days after the wazir's forces had successfully besieged a supposedly impregnable fortress, the picture given to Tavernier was one of considerable power. The ruthless administrator and victorious general, also having a strong interest in diamonds, flattered Tavernier. The merchant was shown five little bags of small gems, which represented a year's production from one of Mir Jumla's mines, worked by 12,000 men. Tavernier did not think much of the jewels, and said so; in his opinion, stones of such poor quality and quantity were neither worth selling nor producing. Mir Jumla agreed with him and immediately sent orders for the mine to be closed.

Tavernier's departure from Aurangzeb's palace in Shahjahanabad was delayed a little; he was happy to wait, though, for the emperor wished to honour him in several unusual ways. Within three days the celebrations for the emperor's birthday were due to begin; Aurangzeb invited

Tavernier to stay and attend the festival, a rare distinction for a European. And his next invitation was unique: he offered to let Tavernier inspect his throne, and the choicest jewels of his treasury. The merchant was delighted.

The next morning Tavernier waited restlessly at the caravanserai, and before long ten officers from the palace came to announce that the emperor was ready to see him. Arriving at the palace, Tavernier was escorted through the courts and corridors that had become so familiar to him – the first court, where the nobles could enter on their elephants; the long passage where the horseguards lived; the second court, with the emperor's bodyguard assembled; and then the third court, with the emperor's hall of audience. This, the 'hall of forty pillars', was raised a few feet above the level of the court and surrounded by marble columns and arches. One of the emperor's lesser thrones stood in the centre of the pillared hall, facing the court; before it, on the lower level, were the seats of the four secretaries of state. There, too, the courtiers would gather, and musicians would play 'sweet and pleasant sounds'. Across the centre of the court, a small channel ran from one side to the other. Strangers were not allowed beyond this until summoned by the emperor; everyone, however illustrious, had to await his call there.

Tavernier was led through here by two of the custodians of the royal jewels. One was a Persian, the other a Banian, and Tavernier did not like either of them. Both had arrived at court earlier that same year and had ingratiated themselves so much to Aurangzeb that he gave them the office of custodians, which meant that they were entitled to see all jewels offered to the emperor for sale or as presents before he did, as Mir Jumla did for the King of Golkonda. But the unscrupulous pair would attempt to buy everything cheaply for themselves, intending to make a profit when they passed goods on to the emperor; and when Tavernier refused to comply with this practice, they contrived to make him lose 10,000 rupees on one of his sales.

The unpleasant pair presented Tavernier to the emperor, and then led him to a small open chamber at one end of the hall. The chief of the royal treasury greeted the merchant, and gave a signal; four eunuchs entered. They carried two large wooden trays covered with gold leaf, and on the trays lay fifty separate jewels.

The two custodians had to count everything three times over, then scribes came and listed all the jewels. It was the usual patient Indian way of doing things, but seeing the trays of gems, poor Tavernier became very impatient, feeling that the Persian and the Banian were taunting him.

At last the chief of the treasury gave him the first one. It was the

'Great Mogul', the diamond presented to Shah Jahan by Mir Jumla from the mine of Kollur. Tavernier called it 'a splendid stone – a round rose, with a beautiful water'. He weighed it carefully; it measured on the scales 319½ *ratis*, in Indian weights, or 280 carats. This surprised him very much – the stone presented to Shah Jahan had weighed 900 *ratis*, or 787½ carats. But he was assured it was the same one. The enormous loss in weight had come about because the original stone had had several flaws, and the emperor, wishing for these to be concealed, entrusted the stone to a Venetian cutter living in court. The man, Hortensio Borgio, was so clumsy in his work that he simply ground the stone down and down. Since the whole Indian idea was to maintain the stone's weight as nearly as possible, the emperor was not at all pleased. Borgio had not even cut the lost parts off; then, at any rate, they could have stood as separate jewels. In the hands of the incompetent Venetian, nearly two thirds of the 'Great Mogul' diamond had vanished into powder. It is hardly surprising that Borgio was not paid for his labours – indeed, he was lucky to get away with a fine of 10,000 rupees.

However, the emperor himself was at least partly responsible for the diminution of the diamond; he had an abundance of other cutters available, who, being Indian, could have understood his wishes far better, and who were in any case more skilled than Borgio. Tavernier was of the opinion that European cutters in general had much to learn from the Indians, and he lamented the damage done as much as the Indians did; but everyone agreed it was still a magnificent jewel.

Now, though Tavernier's journals of his six voyages are sometimes a little contradictory, occasionally rather obscure and at times obviously written from hearsay rather than first-hand observation, his description of the 'Great Mogul' is an important point in the story of the Koh-i-noor. He was not an erudite man; he had no subtleties of philosophy to offer; his accounts of Indian history are mostly borrowed from Bernier; and if, in his engagingly simple way, he loved grandeur and the aura of nobility much as a child loves dressing-up, nevertheless he had one area of authority, clarity and reliability. Diamond dealing was his profession, and without a doubt his notes on the 'Great Mogul' are accurate and trustworthy.

In the latter half of the nineteenth century, the presentation of the Koh-i-noor to Queen Victoria and the general interest in things Indian prompted several English historians to investigate the various famous diamonds of India. Babur's diamond, the 'Great Mogul' and the Koh-i-noor were the three of most interest, and a majority of English accounts attempted to show that either Babur's diamond was the Koh-i-noor, or that the 'Great Mogul' was, or that all three jewels were one and the same. There was a great deal of confusion, caused by variations in weights and measures, by the interpretation of the vague stories as precise records, and above all by that too-frequent failing of historians: the wish to make historical evidence fit a pet theory, however ill-becoming the match. Tavernier's records and reputation suffered much at that time, with his notes being accepted or rejected in a very cavalier fashion, the criterion for their acceptability being whether or not they filled a particular historian's hypothesis.

One hypothesis that was a favourite with many was that all the three great historical diamonds were identical. This theory had two roots: there was the coincidence of weight between Babur's diamond – 186 carats – and the weight of the Koh-i-noor when it arrived in England; and, more importantly, there was the emotional attraction to the Empire-builders of the idea that a diamond should be associated with imperial rule for so long.

But if the attractive proposition was to be maintained, all of Tavernier's careful notes had to be ignored. Aurangzeb, the Great Mogul himself, would have to be mistaken in saying that the diamond came from Mir Jumla; Tavernier's weighing of the jewel would have to be totally inaccurate; and the drawing he himself made of the jewel had to be considered inconsistent with his written description of it. In fact, to unite all three diamonds in one identity, the only point that *could* be acknowledged was that Tavernier had seen a large diamond. Everything else he noted had to be thrown out.

Such treatment of professional and undoubtedly precise notes was shoddy, to say the least. The historians contradicted each other and even contradicted themselves. One scholar, Edwin Streeter, wrote a book called *Great Diamonds of the World*; in one edition, he reported that 'all are agreed' that the Koh-i-noor was identical with Babur's diamond, the 'Great Mogul' being a different stone; another edition of the same book said, with an air of definition, 'any doubt as to the Mogul and Koh-i-noor being *identical* is but rarely entertained'.

A doctor with the charming name of Valentine Ball came to the rescue. In 1889, he published an English translation of the *Six Voyages*, with copious notes and appendices. In an appendix he made a thorough comparative analysis of the certain facts relating to the various diamonds. He had no preconceived theories to fill; he was simply exasperated by the contradictions and muddled thinking of his contemporaries, and was particularly indignant about their treatment of Tavernier's records. After a clear and lengthy study of the available definite information, he came to this conclusion:

Tavernier's account of the Mogul's diamond has, I think, been fully proved in the preceding pages to be quite inapplicable to Babur's diamond, while all his facts and the balance of probability favour the view that in the Koh-i-noor we are justified in recognizing the Mogul's diamond. This . . . is consistent with the literal acceptance of all of Tavernier's statements, and with the physical condition of the Koh-i-noor when it came to Europe, but of none of the other theories can the same be said.

Ball was quick to acknowledge that his theory, though based on fact rather than romantic supposition, was still only a theory – but, in the best tradition of scientific investigation, it was formed from the facts, and fitted them all.

Yet the rumblings of disagreement were not quite stopped. In 1897, in the British Museum, an old manuscript came to light which related how Babur's diamond had found its way through various owners until it ended up in the Deccan. The information was publicized by a Mr H. Beveridge, a member of the Royal Asiatic Society, who commented rather smugly that 'Professor Ball did not know this'; and it was enough to start the romantic conjecture all over again. Beveridge guessed that Mir Jumla had obtained the stone somehow, though there was nothing to suggest it; he also contrived to forget that Mir Jumla's presentation stone was far bigger than Babur's.

On the coincidence of weight between Babur's jewel and the Koh-i-noor on its arrival in England, Ball had already pointed out a fact which many people chose to ignore: there was yet another diamond of the same weight, in the treasury of the Shah of Persia. This was known as the Darya-i-noor, the 'Ocean of Light', and Ball wrote: 'I have in vain sought for any well-authenticated fact which in the slightest degree controverts or even throws doubt on the suggestion that the Darya-i-noor may very possibly be Babur's diamond.'

Probably no one will ever know for certain one way or the other. History, it has been said, is a set of agreed lies; it can be very confusing when disagreement sets in. But there is no reason to doubt Tavernier's statements concerning the 'Great Mogul', and on the whole it seems extremely probable that the jewel shown him by order of Aurangzeb was indeed the Koh-i-noor.

One by one the other royal jewels passed from the chief of the treasury to the merchant. He examined each one, weighing them and assessing their quality. There were more diamonds, pear-shaped or square, and jewels set with many diamonds; there were pear-shaped pearls, round pearls and pearl buttons. There was a chain of pearls and rubies, another of pearls and emeralds, and there were amethysts, sapphires and single rubies. Tavernier noted the details of every gem; he took his time, delighting as much in the honour bestowed on him as in the jewels themselves. Aurangzeb, unlike his forebears, was not fond of pomp and display. Tavernier knew that the distinction vouchsafed him was not only unique among Europeans, it was also extremely rare among Indians, and he loved it.

The delight continued: after the jewels, the thrones; there were seven of them. He examined them all. The first and by far the most magnificent was the legendary Peacock Throne.

'It resembled, in form and size, our camp beds,' said Tavernier, 'being about six feet long and four feet wide.' But there the resemblance to a camp bed ended. The throne was raised on legs two feet high; these were joined by the bars that made the base of the throne, and from the bars sprang twelve pillars, rising from the throne's back and sides to support a pyramidical canopy above it. Feet and bars alike were covered with gold, and were further embellished with diamonds, rubies and emeralds. The centre of each bar was decorated with one large ruby with four emeralds set around it, forming a quincunx; then, from each central quincunx, others radiated along each bar, made alternately of rubies around emeralds, then emeralds around rubies. In all there were 108 rubies, together with 116 emeralds. Though several of both were flawed, they were all of good size; Tavernier estimated they weighed up to 60 carats – and what was more, 'the least of the diamonds on the throne weighs 100 carats, and some weigh apparently 200 or more'.

The pyramidical canopy, too, was hung with diamonds and pearls, and every one of the columns below it was surrounded with rows of perfectly round pearls, all of fine water; but the most gorgeous part of the whole creation, perched on the apex of the pyramid, was the bird that gave the throne its name.

The peacock's body was of solid gold, inlaid with precious stones; in the centre of its breast was another large ruby, with a pear-shaped pearl hanging from it. The tail was a massive, fully extended fan of blue sapphires.

On either side of the bird stood a bouquet of flowers of the same height; many different blossoms were represented, and all were of gold inlaid with jewels.

Dizzy with such magnificence, Tavernier, much as he loved splendour, found it hardly worthwhile to mention the other six thrones, which were all smaller, and covered in diamonds. 'One may become disgusted with the most beautiful things when they are too often before one's eyes,' he commented. Yet the feast still continued – for five days the birthday celebrations went on. Preparations had been going along for two months, with vast tents of gold and velvet being erected within the palace. One of the central ceremonies was the solemn weighing of the emperor. 'If he should weigh more than the previous year,' said Tavernier, 'the rejoicing is so much the greater' – a natural reaction, for the custom was that the emperor should be weighed against gold, which was distributed among the people afterwards. Aurangzeb, however, contrived to avoid this. His nobles and admirers, for their part, could not avoid giving the customary presents and tributes to him – he received elephants, camels, horses, carpets, gold and silver. The days passed in a whirl of ceremony and a dream of lavish stateliness for the French diamond merchant; but he kept his business head sufficiently to estimate the value of the birthday presents. Thirty million *livres* was his reckoning – or around £20 million sterling.

Having left Shahjahanabad at last, the merchant-traveller continued his last journey around Asia for four years more; he went to Bengal, Agra and Surat. His final return to Europe was again by the overland route through Constantinople. It was December 1669 when he eventually arrived in Paris. He was welcomed there by the king, Louis XIV, and shortly afterwards was granted a title of nobility. It was the highest point of his life, and the crest continued for several years. He wrote the account of his six voyages as a record of personal experience and things observed. It was an unpretentious book and extremely popular. There were ten editions during his lifetime, and a further thirteen over the following century; it was translated into English, Dutch, Italian and German. It contained not a speck of philosophy, and Voltaire thought it was contemptible, but it still continued to sell.

In 1684, when Tavernier was seventy-nine years old, the Elector of Brandenburg asked him if he would become his ambassador to India. It would have been the perfect end to the old traveller's life. In his journeys he had come to love India as much as his own country; he was liked and respected in each, and knew the Indian way of life in court and country better than almost any other European. The Elector also wanted him to head a commercial company for further Indo-European trade, and Tavernier accepted the appointment. He sold both his estate and his barony of Aubonne to obtain capital for the future business; and then he entrusted a cargo of goods worth 222,000 francs to his nephew, who was sailing for India. The profit expected from the sale of these goods was in the region of a million livres. Whether or not it was actually realized is uncertain, but Tavernier never saw either the goods or his nephew again.

Eventually word reached the old man that his nephew had settled in Persia. Tavernier, by this time eighty years old, was in no mood to let him stay there, and went to Paris to organize a journey of recovery. While he was there, the Elector began to have second thoughts about the advisability of a commercial company to India, and cancelled the whole project. In France, Louis had revoked the Edict of Nantes, effectively ridding himself of his Nonconformist subjects. It is said that Tavernier, a Protestant of Protestant parentage, found himself in January 1686 incarcerated in the Bastille.

Eighteen months later, in July 1687, he obtained a passport to Switzerland at a cost of 30,000 *livres*. From Switzerland he set out on his seventh journey to the East, and nothing more was heard of him for the best part of 200 years.

In 1885, a man named Tokmakof was looking around an old Protestant cemetery near Moscow. One of the tombstones bore a partly obliterated date: '16 . . .', and the name in full: 'Jean-Baptiste Tavernier'. Tokmakof was intrigued. He investigated further and learned that the traveller had come through Sweden, and then in early February 1689 had arrived in Russia. Probably no one will ever know why he went there; perhaps he simply felt too old to go chasing off to Persia. He was over eighty; he had travelled all round Europe, and further through Asia than almost any of his contemporaries, but he had never been to Russia. It is a romantic thought, but probably true to say that, after a lifetime of journeying, in which he had been honoured by two of the most powerful kings in the world, the old merchant simply decided to keep on travelling till the end.

Three

Trade's Increase

The birth of the East India Company – its early days – the English and Portuguese in India – Sivaji Raja – the progress of the company – Shah Jahan – Aurangzeb – the beginnings of the decline of the Mogul Empire

One chilly December day in the early seventeenth century, a large crowd was gathering in a shipyard in Deptford, which at the time was a village a few miles south-east of London. It was going to be a great day: His Majesty King James I of England and VI of Scotland was to be present at the launching of a new vessel. For many months the yard had rung with the sound of saws and curses, but at last the ship was ready. She was the largest craft yet built in England – 1,100 tons of oak – but that was not the only reason for the king's presence on the occasion. It would have been obvious had the vessel been a warship, yet the great mass that towered in the dry-dock, dwarfing the men busy around her keel, was destined to be a merchantman. The king was there because English commercial horizons had been expanding rapidly, and as monarch, able to tax imports, he had a special interest in them; and the owners of the new ship had a special interest in him. The ship was no Channel coaster; she was the flagship of a small fleet due to set sail early in the New Year, on the long voyage around Africa to the Spice Islands in the East. Her name was the *Trade's Increase*.

Aboard the ship, as she lay in her dry-dock awaiting the rising tide, a lavish party was going on. The owners of the vessel, a group of merchants, wanted to impress the king, and as he sat at table he was able to see things rare even for royal eyes: plates and goblets of gold and silver brought from another world – the distant, unreal world of India – and now owned by the men who sat proudly around him – the governor and directors of the East India Company.

The company had been formed a decade earlier, under a charter granted by Queen Elizabeth on the last day of the old century. The charter, which gave them the monopoly in England of 'traffic and merchandise to the East Indies', still had six years to run by the spring of

1609, but the canny merchants had already managed to have it renewed. The company had run five voyages, all of which had been enormously profitable. The first had brought back over a million pounds'-weight of pepper; the second had given a return on capital of just under 100 per cent; and the third had returned the staggering figure of 234 per cent – one ship's cargo, bought for less than £3,000, was sold for more than £36,000. Naturally, a certain percentage of these amounts went to the royal purse, but James was a peaceable and cautious man, lacking the fire and verve for exploration that had marked Elizabeth, and his charter to the company included the proviso that the Crown could repeal its favour with three years' notice; so the men of the company wanted to provide a good display. And everything seemed to be going well: the king was in an excellent humour, and had presented the governor, Sir Thomas Smythe, with a jewelled gold chain.

Flags and bunting blew in the wind; formal speeches were read; and then should have come the moment that every sailor and shipwright knows and awaits, the moment when ship and water meet for the first time – the nervous expectant hush, then the hilarity of relief, the cheers and handshakes as the craft rises buoyantly up. But the launch was a failure. Though the king had given the ship her name, there had been one mistake which no king could undo. Someone had miscalculated the height of the tide, and there simply was not enough water in the dry-dock to get the ship afloat. She sat there, stolid and unmoving. His Majesty was surprised, and then annoyed, at the anticlimax, and when it became apparent that the *Trade's Increase* was just not going to move without a great deal of effort, the king left.

Several days later, after a lot more work, the ship finally floated. Perhaps she sat a little heavily on the tide, looking rather cumbersome, but she certainly did not wallow; she had been built with all the expertise that English boat-builders could muster, and, with great relief, the men who had made her congratulated each other.

After the anticipatory build-up of the party and the fiasco of the launch, Sir Thomas, sporting his new gold chain, and his directors must have felt very apprehensive. Such a bad impression of the company was bound to influence the king. But they need not have worried – the charter was not revoked, despite James's discontented departure. Indeed, it was renewed, again and again, over nearly 300 years, until the company was finally wound up in 1874.

It is a big jump from the heat and dust of India, the elegance and splendour of the Mogul court, and the poverty and squalor of the peasants, to the cold wet mists of the Thames in winter; but as the aptly named *Trade's Increase* finally creaked out of her dry-dock that dismal

December, more than the launching of a ship was taking place. Unwittingly and unintentionally, the most extensive empire the world has seen was germinating; and the symbolic climax of its growth would be the possession of the Koh-i-noor.

There are two aspects of the East India Company which are immediately striking. The first is the immense size to which it grew; at its zenith it controlled a fifth of the population of the world – and this, it must be remembered, was as a commercial company. The second aspect is that for at least the first generation of its existence, the men of the company never had any intention of winning imperial dominion. Their interest was purely in trade, and it was a long time before they discovered that the idiosyncrasies of Indian trading life were leading them into the position of rulers. How this happened, and where and why, and who made it happen – these questions are the theme of this chapter.

There were four European nations closely involved with Indian trade: the French, the Dutch, the English and the Portuguese. The Portuguese got there first, in 1498; by 1529, the French had probed as far as Sumatra; and in 1597, after a round voyage of two and a quarter years, Cornelius de Houtman brought a cargo of pepper from Bantam to Holland. This so excited the Dutch that in the following year they sent twenty-two ships on the eastern route; and it excited the English as well. In the summer of 1602, the ships of the East India Company's first voyage, under command of James Lancaster, anchored off the north of Sumatra.

Altogether there were five ships, and all of them were tiny by modern standards – the largest was only 600 tons, and the others were 300 tons or less. An interesting detail is that the hulls of the four largest vessels were coated with cement, to proof them against worms. The fifth ship was simply a supply-carrier; after five months at sea, when her cargo had been consumed, she was set adrift.

The late-coming English were after the same thing as all the others: spices, particularly pepper, to enliven their tedious northern diets. But they soon discovered that it was not just a matter of sailing out, trading and sailing back again; the Portuguese were well-established, the Dutch had enormous financial backing, both were shifty and vicious towards each other and the English, and neither had the slightest intention of allowing the English to encroach on territory they regarded as their own. Added to this was the question of oscillating alliances and hostilities at home; news of any change took a year or more to reach the distant traders. Among the native populations, the Portuguese put it about that the English were cannibals, and it became part of every voyage in the company's ships to fight either the Dutch or Portuguese or both. Undoubtedly the company would have preferred to have traded peacefully, but somewhat to their surprise they never had the chance. Once they realized this – and it did not take long – they joined in the general mêlée with a will; for example, Lancaster himself waylaid and looted a Portuguese galleon on the very first voyage. The combination of Dutch and English effectively ousted the old Portuguese monopoly in the Spice Islands, and once that was achieved, the sheer superiority of numbers on the Dutch side meant the English had to move on. Early in 1623, the Dutch govenor at Amboyna in the Moluccas arrested, tortured and executed ten Englishmen trading on the island. It was later acknowledged that the charges against the English had all been false, and Anglo-Dutch relations took half a century to improve; but the English got the message: they were not wanted in the Spice Islands. And so they went to India.

India was at that time weaving its way through the dissolute reign of Jahangir, the 'World-Grasper', son of Akbar the Great and father of Shah Jahan. The period of his rule (1605–28) was the first time the East India Company really got to grips with India; and a very frustrating time it was.

Individual merchants like Tavernier fitted in quite well with Indian ideas and experience. With the nascent trading companies of Europe, however, an element entered Indian life that was completely foreign. Where Tavernier and others like him were perfectly happy to be subject to Indian trading habits, the companies, and the East India Company in particular, wanted something very different. They were not trading as individuals, but as representatives of a nation; and as such they wanted to trade by treaty – and at first this seemed to be very nearly impossible. The law in India could be made and unmade by the emperor at his slightest whim; he, after all, was above the law, and it was inconceivable that he should bind himself permanently to an agreement with anyone. This was especially true with Jahangir, whose addiction to opium and alcohol made him subject to wildly variable moods. Besides the basic antipathy towards the idea of trading treaties, the company had another hurdle to contend with: the Portuguese had had representatives in and around the Mogul court for years, who did everything they possibly could to interfere. Intrigue and deception were the order of the day for the Portuguese; for the Moguls (when they showed any interest at all) it was a question of trying to assess the truth and worth of the Europeans' accounts of one another, without committing themselves irrevocably to either side. The English reply to each was a mixture of bluff and tenacity, and in the end it worked; but it took a very long time, and wearied the lives of many company men.

It is most important to remember the Mogul point of view. Here were they, enjoying the fruits of Akbar's former reign (Jahangir in particular enjoyed himself ceaselessly), with an efficient administration that pleased most of the people who could do anything about it. Then, without warning, many groups of foreigners appeared on their shores, trying to sell thick heavy woollen cloth and wanting spices in exchange. The cloth was interesting as a novelty, but completely impractical for the climate. There were no apparent benefits coming to India, so it is not surprising if the Moguls did not at first take the foreigners seriously.

But both the Portuguese and the English had one thing which the Moguls had not and which they needed; and since it was an advantage in common between the Europeans, the story began to turn on the question of which side would use it better. This one thing was a skilled sea-force; the Moguls had none, and they needed one to protect their trade with the Red Sea and – even more important – to protect the Moslem pilgrims on the route to Mecca.

The Portuguese had held sea-power through most of the Indian Ocean for a full century before the East India Company was even founded, and as early as 1512 they began to administer the native population around Goa. But their spectacular brutality towards Hindus and Moslems, who were regarded as infidels, and towards Christians outside the Roman church, did nothing to endear them either to the natives or to Protestants; and after 100 years, the management of their farflung empire, in which a letter could take a year to reach its destination, was proving hard to bear. At the end of November 1612, an incident took place on the waters off Surat that epitomized the differences between Portuguese and English.

It was the company's tenth voyage. There were two vessels, the 600-ton *Dragon*, a veteran from the first voyage, and the *Hosiander*, a much smaller pinnace. Surat, on the northern part of India's west coast, was a major trade centre. When the Portuguese heard of the two impertinent intruders, they promptly sent a fleet up from Goa to repel them. Four of their enormous galleons lumbered up the coast, with no less than twenty-five frigates to back them. There was an engagement on 29 November, when the *Dragon* took on the Portuguese alone and 'gave each of them a broadside and a brave volley of shot which made them give way and no more come near her that day'. The fight was resumed in the morning, and the *Hosiander* joined in with obvious delight; for 'the fiery *Dragon* bestirring herself, in some three hours hot fight drove three of the galleons on the sands and then the *Hosiander*, drawing little

Various aspects of the East India Company:

The Old Court House, Calcutta

The company's coat of arms

Bombay Green

East India House, Leadenhall Street, London

Nadir Shah who won the diamond from Mohammed Shah in 1739 (see pages 85 to 87)

Mohammed Shah

The Shalimar gardens, Kashmir

Europeans seated in a howdah. By the nineteenth century the Europeans had developed from traders to rulers and took on the appropriate affectations

water, danced the hay about them and so paid them that they durst not show a man on their decks'.

The gleeful account was sent to the company by one of their men involved; and, though the battle was not a major one, it shows the spirit with which the two sides fought. The English, when they could get away from King James, still kept something of the Elizabethan attitude, a youthful exuberance and light-hearted energy, that gave them dominance over the ponderous Portuguese. The one side had a lot to gain, little to lose, and were perfectly willing to 'dance the hay' about forces far larger than their own; the Portuguese mistakenly relied on weight of numbers. The whole thing is reminiscent of earlier land battles in India, like the one between Babur and Ibrahim Lodi.

In itself, the battle of Surat was not a turning-point; it was one of many encounters, greater or lesser, which together gradually switched the balance of power. But it serves as an illustration of the taste of things at sea; and on land, the old balance was shifting as well. Jahangir reeled on till he was sixty-three, and then finally lost his grasp on the world in 1627; and in the same year a baby called Sivaji was born. He was not a Mogul, but a Mahratta, the son of a chief in the territory of Maharashtra. This covered roughly the west and centre of India, from the Narbada river as far south as Goa, and only the northern half of it was included in the Mogul empire. The people were mercenaries, fighting for whomsoever would pay; on occasion they fought for the Mogul, at other times against him. Many of the Mogul emperors had long lives, and the entire remaining three quarters of the seventeenth century saw the accession of only two new emperors, Shah Jahan and Aurangzeb; but despite their longevity and their individual greatness, the empire during that time fell into decline – and Sivaji was one of the reasons for this happening.

By the 1630s, the early years of Shah Jahan's reign, the East India Company was comfortably settled in Surat. The port had become the centre of its operations in India, starting from a simple 'factory', or storehouse for goods, and gradually developing until there were about two dozen merchants in permanent residence. These led a very innocent way of life in those early days: prayers were said regularly; there was no violence to speak of; and though they experimented with arrack, the fiery spirit, and punch, and 'a kind of beer made of coarse sugar, pleasant to the taste and wholesome, but many times water', nevertheless their usual drink was tea. Life was formal and often very short – in 1633, over a six-month period, fourteen of the group of twenty-one died. But while they lived, they showed a healthy interest in the habits of the people around them; they ate curry, kedgeree and mangoes along with their beef and mutton, and 'fine white bread of wheat'; their meals and conversations took place sitting on carpets and cushions; and when they went out, they wore turbans and went on horseback, 'it being the custom of the city'. In behaving thus, these pioneers were far more sensible than many of their descendants; less conscious of their own 'honour' before the native population, they could adopt things like turbans – comfortable and suitable to the climate – without 'losing face'.

On the other coast, the coast of Coromandel, whose name breathes romance, the company made comparable progress. They were granted a tiny tract of land, a mile wide and six miles long, and there they founded Madras. This was the first place that they held in sovereignty, in practical terms. Though they paid an annual tribute to the local raja, they had soldiers to defend it and administered justice to European and Indian alike. Madras began in 1639, and by that time, though the main aim was still trade pure and simple, the company men had begun to understand some of the strings attached to simple trading, Indian style; diplomacy and strength were as vital as cash and goods. In the proper sense of the word, the company men were learning cunning.

This was something that the Portuguese, with their crusading intolerance, never really learned at all. More by luck than good judgement they had managed to avoid any really serious involvement with Indian rivalries, and, not unnaturally, they had no particular wish to become too closely linked with them at all. But, unfortunately for them, backing no one sometimes turned out to be as bad as backing a loser. After Jahangir had been around for a long time, Shah Jahan grew impatient and asked the Portuguese to join him in a rising against the emperor. The Portuguese rather myopically refused, and when Shah Jahan was secure on the throne, he took the opportunity to massacre the men and kidnap the women of the Portuguese factory at Hughli, in Bengal. This was in 1632; the English, keeping a cautious weather-eye open, moved into the area, and in 1651 started their own factory there.

The next major development was a curious volte-face: Charles II married the Portuguese princess, Catherine of Braganza, in 1662, and thenceforward the erstwhile arch-enemies, Portugal and Britain, were allies and ostensibly friends. By then it was almost a reflex action on each side to cut the throat of the other at the earliest opportunity, and the habit took a little while to die out; but, apart from an ally, the company also gained one immensely useful property: the island of Bombay. The island lies a little south of Surat, back on India's north-west coast. In 1668, King Charles leased it to the company, who were mightily pleased with their acquisition, because now Sivaji was on the scene – no longer the mewling infant prince, but a chieftain with the euphonious title of Sivaji Raja; and he was determined to spread his name as far as possible. He opened a guerrilla war with all neighbours who would come within bowshot, including the Mogul, and in 1664 he sacked Surat. The English factory was the only building which did not fall to him, and the company carried on regardless; but when the freebooting raja repeated his exercise in 1670, they decided they had outstayed their welcome. Headquarters were shifted to the island. There the English found, for the first time, independence of all the mainland powers, and Bombay as we know it today was born.

Calcutta came next, created in 1689 by the redoubtable Job Charnock, a florid, eccentric and very determined character. Among a wealth of other achievements, this formidable person rescued a Brahmin widow from the flames of her husband's funeral pyre, then married her himself. By all accounts they lived very happily, and after she died, Charnock sacrificed a cock to her every year; and from his collection of huts on a marshy and pestilential shore grew one of the largest cities in the world.

In the meantime, his colleagues in Bombay exhibited once more their talent for telling which way the wind was blowing and began negotiating with Sivaji. They found him a startling and very refreshing contrast to the Moguls; not only was he interested in their trade proposals, but he agreed swiftly to every important one. What was more, he kept his word. Without doubt he, too, was an opportunist, but after the prima donna vacillating of the temperamental Jahangir, and the touchy autocracies of Shah Jahan and Aurangzeb, the rebellious raja's businesslike attitude must have been a great relief.

The first century of the East India Company's presence in India tends to seem like a swift, unopposed success story. By the end of the seventeenth century, it had established the great trading triangle of Bombay, Madras and Calcutta, with all the paraphernalia of organized life, civil, military and commercial; they had a great number of factories throughout India; and from supplicants at the imperial court they had become a pivot of power between Mogul and Mahratta. But, reading the story of a hundred years, it is easy to forget that it could not all be seen in the same perspective at the time. One has to remember all the people who never knew the rest of the story, but who only knew one tedious dawn rising after another, as they set out once more to try and win the emperor's favour, or dreamed in the hot sticky nights of the homeland they would never see again.

*

From the plough to the plough is seven generations, according to an old proverb. The Emperor Aurangzeb was of the sixth generation of Mogul rule. It was he who showed the Koh-i-noor to Tavernier, and he who brought almost the whole of India within the Mogul empire. He was also the last of the Great Moguls, and he ruled for a full fifty years. But though he extended the bounds of his empire greatly, it was paradoxically he who caused the downfall of Mogul India. The reason lies in one word: autocracy.

The tale of Aurangzeb's accession is among the most famous stories of fratricide ever told. Late in 1657, Shah Jahan had fallen seriously ill, and this immediately ignited a war of succession between his four sons. By and by the emperor recovered and announced in no uncertain terms that he was well again; but his sons took no notice. They carried on fighting, until eventually Aurangzeb defeated all the other three, killing two of them and imprisoning his father, and then embarking on half a century of conquest and conversion – or attempted conversion. Unity without uniformity had been the keynote of Akbar's reign. By comparison, the extension of Mogul rule under his grandson Aurangzeb was a hollow achievement, for the new territories were never part of the organic whole; they were only military occupations. Aurangzeb was the most militantly Moslem of all the Moguls; his deep religious conviction manifested itself in a wave of anti-Hindu iconoclasm and oppression. Temples were destroyed and desecrated; the tax on non-Moslems was reintroduced after more than a hundred years of abeyance; by every means possible, Hindus were made into second-class people.

There were two things about which Aurangzeb cared passionately: his religion and his empire. He pursued both with single-minded intensity and terrific vigour; he was genuinely pious and also very brave, leading every campaign in person if possible, even after he was over eighty. But his great failing was that he wanted to do everything himself, and he wanted everyone to agree with him. A unity of that sort was politically and religiously impossible, and ultimately Aurangzeb was a lonely and pathetic failure. The fusion of Moslem and Hindu cultures, for which Akbar had striven so long and with such success, had been under severe strain ever since his death, and Aurangzeb managed to destroy it altogether. His religious intolerance alienated his millions of Hindu subjects irrevocably; his autocratic rule took away the spirit of initiative in his ministers and viceroys. It was true that in the end he was nominal ruler of almost the whole of India – only the southernmost tip of the sub-continent remained completely independent – and in that sense he was a *chakravartin* in a way none had been before him. But he would have been the first to admit that over most of the land his rule was in name only. The southern states remained defiantly Hindu, and in the north Rajput clans, and the Jat tribes south of Delhi, were constantly rebellious. Sivaji's success, too, largely resulted from his role as a focus for Hindu resentment.

An all-India empire was possible, but an all-Moslem India was not. A land so large and diverse could not be held together by one man, no matter how strong his personal beliefs. Indeed, if Aurangzeb's beliefs had been less strong or less narrow – if he had been prepared to compromise, or able simply to tolerate his Hindu people – then the Mogul empire would quite possibly have continued to flourish.

Aurangzeb died in 1707, eighty-nine years old, worn out with the effort of attempting the impossible. As he was dying, he wrote a touching letter to his favourite son:

> Soul of my soul . . . Now I am going alone. I grieve for your helplessness. But what is the use? Every torment I have inflicted, every sin I have committed, every wrong I have done, I carry the consequences with me. Strange that I came with nothing into the world, and now go away with this stupendous caravan of sin! Wherever I look I see only God. Let not Moslems be slain and the reproach fall upon my useless head. I commit you and your sons to God's care, and bid you farewell. Peace!

'This stupendous caravan of sin' – it was no insensitive tyrant who wrote those words. Aurangzeb ruled as he did because, for him, it was the only way. Yet during his lifetime he knew into what straits his actions were leading the empire, and as he lay dying he foresaw the chaos that would ensue. Indian historians have called the eighteenth century 'the great anarchy'. It is appropriate; in the thirteen years following Aurangzeb's death, there were four emperors, all of whom died in unnatural ways. The part played by Europeans in the fate of India grew rapidly, and the fourth contending nation, France, entered the fray, competing with the English on the east and west coasts. The Afghans, after decades of rebellion, achieved independence; and so did the Sikhs, the Rajputs, the Jats – indeed almost all of India. By the 1770s, all the territory that remained to the Mogul name was a tiny pocket of land extending a few score miles around Delhi, and not even that was inviolate. In 1739, a Persian force sacked the city completely, delivering a mortal blow to the heart of the dying Mogul organism; and as the old unity fell in ruins, the Koh-i-noor vanished from India.

Four

The Shepherd-King

Nadir Quli, the Persian shepherd-boy – condition of Persia in the early eighteenth century – invasions of Russians, Afghans and Turks – an Afghan becomes Shah – Nadir's military flair – he becomes Shah – European opinion – Nadir's invasion of India – the sack of Delhi – Nadir claims and names the great diamond – he returns to Persia – his madness and death

A thousand miles north-west of India, beyond the wild hills and passes of Afghanistan, there is a range of mountains called Allahu Akbar. The peaks rise over 10,000 feet high. They stand in the most northern part of Khorasan, the borderlands of Persia. At the end of the seventeenth century, Persia was rotting, and Khorasan was a poor province peopled by nomadic shepherds. In the summer they would take their flocks to the high pastures, retreating again at the onset of winter to the warmer lowlands. It could be a long migration; one tribe had their summer grazing ground on the south of the Allahu Akbar range, and their winter ground on the lower slopes of the north side. Their southerly summer ground was called Mayab Kubkan, after a group of wells that watered the area.

All through the summer of 1688, as she spun and cooked and herded at Mayab Kubkan, there was one woman who could feel her new baby growing within her. Then autumn came; the days turned colder, and the tribe turned back across the mountains. By the time they reached their winter pasture it was November, and the child, conceived in the passionate spring, was born. His parents were good Moslems, and they named him Nadir Quli – 'Slave of the Wonderful'.

In far-off India, the 'great anarchy' began in 1707, when Aurangzeb was wrapped in his pauper's shroud. At the same time Persia was mouldering under the last Savafid kings. Each generation had become more effete than the last, for the Savafids had solved the problems of wars of succession by closeting their princes in the harem until the moment when they were called upon to rule. To Persian princes, with every natural male appetite, the arrangement seemed quite agreeable; but when the prince became king, he had next to no training for the role. The result was a series of feeble monarchs, largely advised by eunuchs.

In 1718, a trade delegation from Russia reported to Peter the Great. Among their commercial notes, they made pointed remarks about the incompetence of the shah – 'unless he be replaced', they said, 'the ruin of the country is inevitable'. Two years later the Turks came to the same conclusion: the country was well cultivated, prosperous and led by idiots – in short, it was ripe for the plucking.

But it was the Afghans who made the first grab, in 1721, coming in from Kandahar. Then Peter sailed from Astrakhan, across the Caspian, and invaded in 1722; and after a quick debate on whether it was better to attack Russia or to try to take Persia while the opportunity was open, the Turks joined in as well. That was in 1723; and, in the same year, one of the Persian governors proclaimed himself as an independent ruler in Khorasan.

The Afghans arrived at Isfahan, the Persian capital, at about the time Peter was setting sail. They besieged the city, and it was here that Savafid breeding began to tell. The shah's eldest son was hurriedly taken from the harem, made crown prince, and told to get through the Afghan lines to find reinforcements. Unfortunately, he took one look around, then went straight back to the harem and refused to come out. The second son did the same, and only the third – Tahmasp by name – could be persuaded to tackle the problem. But having found a way through the besieging force, Tahmasp rediscovered the pleasure of food and drink, which were both in short supply in the beleaguered city; so eventually the shah gave in, and with his own hand crowned the Afghan chief King of Persia.

It was not an easy crown to wear – Turkey remained very aggressive, and Russia was determined to maintain its new territories. In fact, the new shah went mad within three years and was beheaded by his own men. By then Tahmasp had become somewhat more kingly and had opened negotiations with both Russia and Turkey, intending to drive out the Afghans and place himself on his ancestral throne. He had very few followers, a mere two or three thousand, and most of those felt greater allegiance to their governor, an ambitious man called Fath Ali Khan. Then a rather unexpected and extremely useful ally appeared in Khorasan. The shepherd's son had grown up.

*

Nadir Quli was a big man. The dominant note in all the romances and histories that have been written about him is one of immensity – in his physical size, in his character, in his dreams and his actions. He was about six feet tall, and very strongly built; black-haired and with a bushy black beard, heavily tanned by sun and wind, and with a voice 'so uncommonly loud and strong, that he frequently, and without straining it, gives Orders to his People at above a hundred Yards Distance'. The description was written by William Cockell, an agent of the East India Company. He met Nadir on several occasions, and made a number of pertinent comments about him.

> When on a March, or in the Field, he contents himself to eat, drink, and sleep like a common Soldier, and enures all his Officers to the same severe Discipline. He is of so hardy a Constitution that he has been often known on a frosty night to repose himself on the Ground in the open Air, wrapt up in his Cloak, with only a Saddle for his Pillow . . . He is never happy but when in the Field.

Throughout his life, Nadir's tastes did indeed remain simple – there were only four things which made him happy: in order of importance, they were water-melons, fighting, women and jewels. The first three he knew well from his youth as a shepherd and bandit; the fourth was an acquired taste; and all of them were fulfilled in India.

Nadir had grown up following his father's occupation; with the tribe, he had tramped backwards and forwards across the Allahu Akbar mountains, driving sheep. But he did not like it, and about the age of fifteen he joined the guard of a local governor. Several years went by, during which he made such a brave show that he was promoted to Captain of the Guard; then his father the shepherd died, the governor married his widowed mother, and Nadir married the governor's eldest daughter. This was the first important stage in his life, providing him with an entry into the ruling élite, and when the governor died a few years later, Nadir expected to succeed to his position. But there were local jealousies that prevented him doing so, and in his disappointment he went to join the force of Malik Mahmud – the governor who had claimed Khorasan as his own independent state.

By this time Nadir's ambition was aroused. He saw no good reason for the governor to be ruler of Khorasan, and he saw plenty of reason for himself taking over. However, he failed, and it was this failure that drove him to become a bandit. He was much more successful at this – indeed, much of his later activity has the flavour of banditry about it – and he and Malik Mahmud became open enemies. Nadir was

1 The legendary origin of the Koh-i-noor: Akura reveals the divine gem, the Syamantaka, to Khrishna (see page 21). The painting, which comes from Northern India, dates from A.D. 1525. Two thousand years after it was first written down, the legend of the Syamantaka had lost none of its popular appeal.

2 Babur – poet, gardener, general and founder of the Mogul Empire –
in the *Bagh-i Vafa,* the Garden of Fidelity (see page 40).

3 Fathepur Sikri: in A.D. 1569, after Salim's birth, Akbar began building the 'City of Victory'. Here, dressed in white, he directs operations personally, as *sudras* carry bricks and courtiers with falcons stand and observe (see page 50).

4 Fathepur Sikri: the birth of Akbar's son Salim, who became Jahangir – the 'World-Grasper' – is celebrated with fanfares of trumpets and the beating of drums. Largesse is distributed to the multitude outside the walls while the royal infant and his mother are nursed inside (see page 48).

The Powerless Glory
Despite the steady decline in their real power, the Mogul Emperors of the eighteenth and nineteenth centuries still displayed fabulous wealth. Behind an ostentatious veneer of fine fabrics, jewels and precious metals, the Mogul Empire decayed into puppetry. 5—A wallhanging of delicately painted and dyed cotton (Western India, early eighteenth century). 6—Ivory throne and footstool presented to Queen Victoria by the Rajah of Travencore. 7—A courtier's essential equipment – garments of gold, vases of crystal, ornaments of emeralds, rubies and pearls. 8—The gracing of a courtly head – pearls, rubies and turquoises set in gold (Delhi, eighteenth century).

9 The Grand Hall of Audience in the Palace of the Moguls in Delhi.
The marble walls are inlaid with precious stones.

10 The Jama Masjid, the Great Mosque in Delhi (see page 49). The
scale of the building is shown by the diminutive figures beside it.

11 The Indian display at the Great Exhibition.

12 The Koh-i-noor in its present setting, the central point of the State Crown of Her Royal Highness Queen Elizabeth, The Queen Mother.

learning guerrilla battle tactics quickly, and had already imposed a rigorous discipline on the men with him, when Tahmasp asked him to assist in restoring the Savafids to their former dignity.

The former crown prince had declared himself shah, despite having no territory and few men, and despite the fact that his father had actually confirmed the Afghan as shah. Although it could be that Nadir, in accepting Tahmasp's request, was simply patriotic, it seems more likely that, like Fath Ali Khan, he was linking his force to the Savafids because it was the only possible way to advance himself from local to national status.

Whatever reasons he held privately, Nadir professed complete loyalty to the Savafids and joined with Tahmasp. They had a strained relationship: Tahmasp did not quite trust Nadir, and Nadir found his efforts hampered by the young self-styled shah. Moreover, Fath Ali Khan was at least as ambitious as Nadir, and the pair became bitter rivals; between them, Tahmasp oscillated as weakly as any of his predecessors. The rivalry culminated in Fath Ali's death, when Nadir managed to convince Tahmasp that the khan was a traitor. Fath Ali was no more a traitor than Nadir, but he would certainly have done the same had he found the chance; each man was backing the shah just so far as was personally useful, and chance took Nadir through.

Within the course of only a few years, he found himself raised from a guardsman to being the right-hand man of Persia's hereditary ruler; then, with an Afghan on the throne, the nominal shah completely dispossessed, and his own personal rival dead, Nadir began to use his real abilities and left chance behind. His rigorous discipline began to revive the Persian troops. He engaged the Afghans in a series of battles far from Isfahan, testing the mettle of his men; and his work was so effective that the Persians, who shortly before would have fled at the mere sight of an Afghan, stood firm in these battles, and won.

Once the myth of Afghan invincibility was broken, it was only a matter of time before Isfahan was recovered; and on 16 November 1729 Nadir the shepherd entered the city without any opposition. The Afghans had fled.

A fortnight later, Tahmasp joined Nadir in the capital. Earlier, Nadir had asked him to go to Tehran, ostensibly on state business; in fact, Nadir just wanted the shah out of the way while he recovered Isfahan, since Tahmasp was still as unreliable as ever in his support. He certainly had reasons for complaint, because Nadir would not let him appoint any ministers, saying that their salaries were better spent on maintaining the army; but it could not be denied that Nadir was having tremendous success against the Afghans. Within a year they had been driven out of Persia altogether, and Ashraf, the second Afghan shah, was dead.

It is curious that 'nadir' in English signifies the lowest point of a cycle, for the reign of Nadir Shah, the shepherd-king, restored Persia to its position of a major power. Nadir became the last of the great conquerors of the Middle East, sharing fame with Alexander, Genghis Khan, Tamerlane and Babur. With Tahmasp as the nominal ruler, Nadir, in 1729, sent a message to the Mogul emperor Mohammed Shah, asking him to close the Indian border to Afghan refugees; then, in 1730, the one-time shepherd took his armies on a vigorous campaign against the Turks and recovered all the territories they had invaded. Tahmasp lost most of them once more in the following year, after a disastrous campaign of his own, and, disappointed, began an impressive series of debauches to console himself. Cockell described the shah as 'a Lazy Indolent Manager, a Sott and Sodomite'; Nadir used the incidents as excuses for deposing Tahmasp and placing Tahmasp's son, Abbas III, on the throne. But Abbas III was only eight months old at the time; he needed a regent, and there was not much doubt about who that should be. For four years more Nadir ruled in all but name, regaining all the ancient Persian lands, except for Kandahar. He took many Turks and Afghans into his armies, which were growing steadily stronger and more efficient; at least there were far more foreigners than Persians in the army, and all were intensely loyal to Nadir. The aura of success shone brightly around him, made all the brighter by Tahmasp's futile character; and in 1736 he took the crown.

This had been expected for a long time by everyone; six years before, Cockell, a mere European, had noted that the people, the court and even the king believed that Nadir's only ambition was to achieve the highest point possible in the realm. When he finally did so, not everyone was sure it was a wise step, but it was such an obvious move that no one except Nadir's mother dared speak openly against it, and even she made only a timid suggestion. The old shepherdess had followed in her extraordinary son's wake, and had watched his rise to power with astonishment; when he took the throne, she must have felt he was over-reaching himself, for she

> intreated Nadir Shah, some time after he had seized the King to restore him, not doubting but his Majesty would make him sufficient Amends, by creating him *Generalissimo* for life. He ask'd her 'whether she really thought so?' She told him, 'She did.' Upon which

he smil'd and said, 'If I was an old Woman, perhaps I might be inclined to think so too.'

One can readily imagine the old lady's state of mind; hitherto her boy had been fighting for the old ruling family, and his success could only be admirable. But actually to make himself king – surely that was going too far. Remembering Nadir Quli, the child who had trotted behind the sheep towards Mayab Kubkan, it must have been difficult for his mother to accept the metamorphosis.

The kingdom was not too much for Nadir; he wanted more, much more, and he got it. He maintained his troops by a terrible discipline – 'if any of his General Officers give Ground without being greatly overpowered, he rides up and kills him with a Battle-axe (which he always carries in his Hand) and then gives the Command to the next in Rank' – but he was also scrupulously fair to his men. In addition, he had a great natural tactical talent. Cockell noted that it was 'scarce credible how quick he is in discerning the Odds on either Side, and how active in succouring his Troops'; and it was these three qualities – discipline, fairness and outstanding generalship – that made him such an overwhelming man.

His crown was singularly appropriate: it was a jewelled helmet of gold. At the time of his coronation, Kandahar remained independent, and one of the new shah's first actions was to make peace with Turkey so that he could complete the subjugation of the Afghans. Kandahar was a formidable objective. Nearly a century before, in 1649, Aurangzeb's men had been unable to destroy it even with artillery, for its walls were thirty feet thick. But Nadir won the city, and then virtually razed it to the ground. Some of the citadel still remains – a few pillars and arches, thirty feet or so high – but its defeat was total.

By this time the years of continuous campaigning had almost impoverished Persia. The country was united, and could have been organized economically, but to settle down to a peaceful kingdom was unthinkable for a man like Nadir. He had fought for Persia because fighting was his life. Nevertheless his country needed money; and India had a great deal.

The ancient magic lure was still there – the promise of easy wealth, great territories, and the excitement of battle. It was irresistible. Nadir decided to make his eldest son Viceroy of Persia, and to set off towards India.

He had some slight excuse for going there; his message to the Mogul, requesting him to close the Indo-Afghan border to prevent the flight of refugees, had been ignored, and though Nadir had repeated the request several times, nothing had come of it. So technically, in crossing the Indian frontier, he was simply in pursuit of rebels, and he loudly proclaimed his friendship for India; but at the same time he warned the Mogul not to send any troops against him or he would be compelled to fight. Of course, it was obvious that in pursuing the Afghans the shah's armies were bound to create a considerable nuisance of themselves in India; it was extremely probable that the Indians would resist this; and it was quite likely that the Mogul would feel obliged to come to the aid of his people. But Nadir's warning to the Mogul not to do so, lest war become necessary, was not merely a gloss of legality over his aggressive action; his favourite wife was a Rajput and a Hindu, and he loved her dearly. She felt no loyalty to the Moguls; the tombs and temples that Aurangzeb had desecrated had been those of her people. But the Persian forces were marching through Hindu territory, and for his wife's sake Nadir was prepared to be as moderate as possible.

However, if the conquest of India was an irresistible attraction, the idea that it should be peaceful was unthinkable. Nadir left Kandahar – or rather, the new city of Nadirabad a few miles from the remnants of Kandahar – on 21 May 1738. He went through Ghazni, the old stamping-ground of Mahmud of Ghazni 700 years before. From there the army progressed to Kabul, 'punishing' the Kabulis who resisted them on the way. There were certainly plenty of Afghans around: the Governor of Kabul organized an army of 20,000 to assist his own men. The Persians routed them, and thereafter it was open war. A similar force attempted to defend Lahore, but eventually had to surrender; to avoid being sacked, the city paid a tribute of two million rupees. Nadir still pretended friendship to the Mogul, which by this time was blatantly untrue. Nevertheless, the Mogul did not seem unduly disturbed as yet, and though he was gathering an army, its progress was more like a stroll than a military advance. There were around 80,000 combatants, but they were attended by so many camp followers that the whole mass numbered nearly a million. The vast, clumsy group was like a moving city, thirty miles in circumference; somehow the Moguls had forgotten, during their long residence in India, that such an unwieldy multitude was not the best defence.

In all 10,000 Indians were killed, and 2,000 Persians. The Indians would have been better served had they overcome their chronic problem of using a huge, non-cooperative assembly – personal enmities between commanders were so strong that one sat on his elephant drinking coffee while the battle was going on, and refused to involve his men at all. And Nadir, in the classic manner, managed to panic the Indian elephants with an original and unpleasant method – he tied camels in pairs with wooden platforms in between, and on the platforms put bundles of blazing naphtha.

The battle took place on 24 February 1739, almost exactly nine months after the Persians entered India. Two days later the Mogul emperor abdicated.

The plain of Karnal lies only eighty miles north of Delhi. This was the extent of the Mogul advance in all those months of warning. Having probed so close to the heart, and having received the crown – though there was no formal investiture – there was not the slightest likelihood that Nadir would turn back. Conquered and conqueror moved towards the capital together, Mohammed Shah, the Mogul emperor, following two miles behind Nadir. Outside Delhi, Nadir waited in the Shalimar gardens while Mohammed prepared the city for a stately reception; then, on 20 March, cannon fired a salute and Delhi – Shajahanabad, the Moguls' own creation – opened its gates to the Persian.

A hundred elephants with musketeers on their backs preceded Nadir. The psychological effect on the Indians can be understood in modern terms if one imagines 100 tanks rolling into one's own capital city, with one's own ruler trailing in the rear.

That night Nadir slept in the palace built by Shah Jahan. The next day the *khutba* was read in his name, and coins were struck with the legend: 'The Sultan over the Sultans of the Earth is Nadir the King of Kings, Lord of the Fortunate Conjunction'. He *was* a king of kings; and the astrological phrase 'Lord of the Fortunate Conjunction' was no accident – it had been one of Tamerlane's titles. But only a few hours later, a rumour flashed through the city that Nadir was dead, or else had been imprisoned by Mohammed, and riots began.

To begin with, Nadir did not believe riots were occurring; but when a body of 1,000 musketeers proved unable to quell the disturbances, he ordered his men to stay armed all night, but not to attack the townspeople. By the morning, 3,000 Persians had been killed.

Nadir still would not let his soldiers retaliate. He rode out at dawn to investigate. Someone took a shot at him, killing the officer beside him; and at that, he let the soldiers loose.

> A general Slaughter commenced from that very Place; the Soldiers in an Instant getting upon the Walls and Terraces began to plunder and kill . . . The whole Streets of the Bazar, and the Allies and Wards on all Sides, the Khanum's Bazar, and round about the Jamih Misjidd (the Great Mosque), and the Cotton and Jewellers Bazars, were all plundered, several Places they set on Fire, and whomsoever they

found in the Wards and Houses, Streets, Allies and Shops, Great and Small, Men and Women, they put to the Sword.

Among the horrors occurred an incident which has a particular pathos; one of the townsmen, seeing the soldiers approach his house, killed twenty of his womenfolk rather than let them fall into Persian hands. But the Persians missed his house out; and

> he was so infatuated that finding himself disappointed, he went out, and bringing some of them back, shewed them the way to his own House, telling them there was a good deal of Money and Effects therein. After they had plundered his House, they went on their way without killing him, which so enraged him that he dispatched himself.

The people of Delhi were desperate; some fought wildly, others killed themselves and their families. The gutters literally ran with blood.

It continued for six hours. At three in the afternoon Nadir ordered the slaughter to cease; it did so immediately. Twenty thousand Indians lay dead. It is not really surprising that Nadir ordered the city to be sacked; every conqueror of Delhi had done the same, though none with such ferocity since Tamerlane in 1398. The two points that are surprising are that Nadir refrained from the pillage for so long, and that, having begun, he did not destroy the city utterly, as he had destroyed Kandahar. The only answer that seems reasonable for both is that he did not actually want to sack Delhi.

This supposition is borne out by contemporary accounts, where Nadir is shown to have held back for as long as possible. Apparently his Rajput wife, thinking of her fellow Hindus, had begged him not to attack the citizens. He certainly knew that his troops, with their tough discipline, were far superior to the untrained, panic-stricken civilians; but, pushed beyond his endurance, he gave a terrible lesson. Had he wished, he could have done far worse.

Apart from the physical suffering, the humiliation was equally terrible. The very heart of the decaying Mogul empire had been hit; and, from the heart, the symbol of empire and of unity was taken to Persia.

The loot included gold and silver, money and jewels, furniture and animals, altogether worth some 700 million rupees. Having worn the imperial crown, Nadir returned it to Mohammed Shah – he knew that India was too large for him to rule it himself, but it was still a subtle degradation to be able to return an empire to its defeated ruler. Having sat on the imperial throne, however, the Persian obviously took a liking to that, for among the spoil was Shah Jahan's Peacock Throne; and then – the diamond.

There are various stories about the way in which Nadir actually got hold of the great jewel. One of the most common tales says that Mohammed Shah, having given all his other valuables to Nadir, concealed the diamond in his turban, hoping to keep that at least. Nadir, hearing of this, made public the news that he would return the empire to the Mogul; at the formal transfer of power he embraced the emperor, and then, as a solemn symbol of their friendship, requested that they exchange turbans. It is less fanciful than it may sound, for the custom was fairly common, and it certainly seems more likely than another story, in which Mohammed Shah voluntarily gave the diamond to Nadir, in gratitude for the return of his empire.

But whether the diamond was given or taken, it was then that it was named. Nadir Shah, on seeing it for the first time, was so astonished – so all the stories say – that he exclaimed, 'Koh-i-noor!' and the 'Great Mogul' became the 'Mountain of Light'.

Nadir left Delhi on 16 May 1739. He stopped at the gardens of Shalimar for a day; then the long journey back began in earnest. It was hard. Crossing one river, the Chenab, many men and a quarter of the spoils of Delhi were lost. They went by way of Nadirabad, the new city by old Kandahar, arriving there on 4 May 1740. The round trip had taken just under two years.

In the end, Mohammed Shah did get something out of it all: Nadir sent him 200 camel-loads of his favourite melons. Whether or not the emperor felt it to be a fair exchange is not on record. For his part, Nadir had been quite impressed by the actual city of Delhi; he decided to build a new city in Persia modelled on the Indian capital. When he got back to Persia, he found his son had been ruling very capably in his absence; and whatever doubts people may have had when the shepherd first took the Persian throne were now settled. Cockell echoed the popular feeling:

> As he has performed such Wonders when he had hardly any Money or Men, what may we not expect of him now he is possess'd of so immense a Treasure? 'Tis probable he may live thirty Years longer; and in that Space of Time, if his Designs are attended with the same Success he has hitherto met with, to what Pitch of Grandeur may not a Man of his unbounded Ambition and Courage arrive at?

Such optimism was understandable; Nadir had rescued his country and had been given the crown of India by the emperor's own hand. And with his son's able performance, it seemed that a new great dynasty was being firmly established. 'They who knew the young Man (for I never saw him) judge he'll make full as great a Figure in the World as his Father,' said Cockell. Had the prince lived, so it might have been; and had Nadir died then, he would certainly have been the greatest national hero that Persia had ever seen. But after all the triumphs, the end was sour.

All his life Nadir had been aggressively healthy, but while he was in India he contracted dropsy. To a man with such pleasure in physical activity, any physical restriction was anathema; he became melancholic and would sometimes have uncontrollable outbursts of rage and irrationality. It was during one such outburst, in 1742, that he ordered his eldest son to be blinded with a red-hot wire. His madness grew, and as he sank into insanity, he became increasingly tyrannical; the shepherd-boy who had been king turned into a desperate brooding butchering despot. To have such a king was too high a price for unity; and in the spring of 1747, Nadir was assassinated in his tent at night.

The Golden Temple of the Sikhs at Amritsar

A Victorian view of the Sikh cavalry

Ranjit Singh, the 'Old King', riding a white horse. The right profile hides his blind eye

Lord Wellesley (see page 104)

The diamond in its 'original setting', designed by Ranjit Singh

Portrait heads of Dost Mohammed, Emir of Afghanistan, and three of his family by Emily Eden, 1841

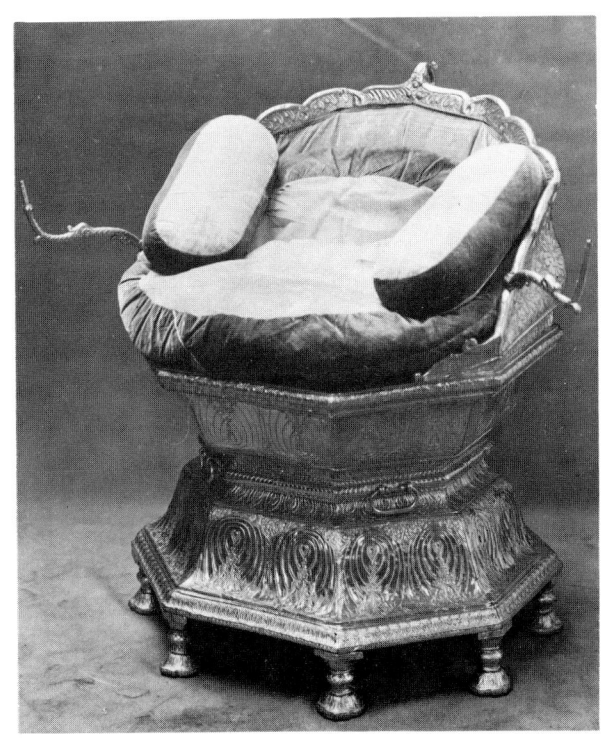

Splendid simplicity: Ranjit's throne

The Battle of Gujerat

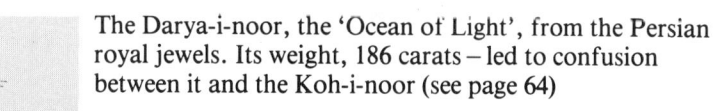

The Darya-i-noor, the 'Ocean of Light', from the Persian royal jewels. Its weight, 186 carats – led to confusion between it and the Koh-i-noor (see page 64)

Scene at the end of the Battle of Delhi

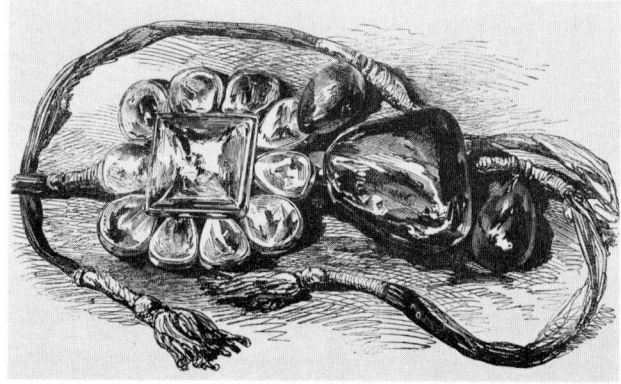

Five

The Boy-King, the Eunuch and the Afghans

Anarchy in Persia – Nadir's grandson Rukh Mirza becomes Shah, is deposed and blinded – varying accounts of the Koh-i-noor – Ahmad Shah Abdali, the first Afghan king – the diamond in Afghanistan – the tyrannical Agha Mohammed Shah – his pursuit and torture of Shah Rukh Mirza – invasion of India by Ahmad Shah – Ahmad's love of Afghanistan – the jewel passes to his son and grandsons – Afghanistan in chaos – the Koh-i-noor is hidden – Ahmad's grandsons, Shuja and Zaman, in exile

The silent white stone travelled, leaving a wake of blood. It would be fanciful to attribute the viciousness that surrounded the jewel to a supernatural quality in the jewel itself; yet precious stones frequently have stories attached to them of curses or blessings, and it is said now that the Koh-i-noor brings bad luck to any man who owns it, but good luck to a woman. When one thinks of its early owners, the idea has an air of reality. Shah Jahan had died in prison, held there by his own son; Aurangzeb had stretched Mogul power to breaking point, and died with an overwhelming sense of sin and guilt; his immediate descendants had been murdered in quick succession; Mohammed Shah, the last Mogul to own the jewel, had seen his empire's capital sacked and ruined by a Persian adventurer; and then the Persian, too, had suffered, descending step by step into madness, leaving pyramids of heads to mark his journey, until at last his own headless body lay still.

When Nadir died, Persian unity collapsed immediately. As news of his death spread through his camp, the Afghan soldiers and the Qizilbash – the red-turbanned Persian horsemen – began to fight, and 4,000 of the Afghans fled back to their mountain homes. The provinces of Azerbaijan, Ghilan, Mazanderan and Georgia announced their independence, and in the prevailing anarchy the Dutch seized Karak, one of Persia's islands in the Gulf. The first few years after Nadir's death were filled with a bewildering spin of would-be monarchs. Ali Quli Khan, Nadir's nephew, took the throne first. He named himself Adil

Shah – 'the Just King' – and straightway slaughtered all possible claimants to the throne except one, Shah Rukh Mirza, Nadir's grandson. The child was spared because he was descended from the Savafids as well as from Nadir, and Ali Quli felt it might be politic to have one Savafid in reserve. But after a few months Ali Quli was dethroned and blinded by his brother Ibrahim; and then, some weeks later, Ibrahim was blinded, and both brothers were killed by their own soldiers. The boy, Shah Rukh, became king.

Very shortly afterwards, another pretender emerged and defeated the king; the child was blinded. One of his generals rose against the pretender, blinded *him* and reinstated Shah Rukh; then an Arab chief and a Kurdish chief decided it was their turn to rule. They joined forces, defeated Shah Rukh's general and, with striking lack of originality, decided he too had seen enough of the world. The practice was habit-forming. Before long, the Arab and the Kurd quarrelled; the Arab won, and the Kurd lost his eyes.

There are differing accounts of the Koh-i-noor at this time. Some say that Ali Quli Khan appropriated it, and that after Shah Rukh's accession the boy owned it in turn. Others say that it remained in Persia, but not in the turbulent provinces. In the south, peace was restored ten years after Nadir's death by Karim Khan, an uneducated but remarkably sensible and humane chieftain of the Zand tribe. Karim fought a good many battles against other pretenders, and lost most of them; but the Persians by this time had had their fill of war, and though he was no great general, the kindliness and good humour of the Zand chief made him popular. Popularity proved more powerful than force of arms, and Karim ruled altogether for twenty-nine years; twenty of these years were completely peaceful. It was a considerable relief for the war-weary country, and it would be pleasant to imagine that the Koh-i-noor was present during this peaceful unity. However, there is a third story telling of the diamond's whereabouts, and on the whole it is this account which seems the most probable.

The Afghans who fled back to their homeland after Nadir's death were led by a man named Ahmad Shah Abdali, who had been one of the most able and most loyal of Nadir's generals. He had learned his profession well in the Persian army, and after his return to Afghanistan he did something that had never been done before: he unified the country.

The idea that Ahmad Shah possessed the jewel is current in two forms. One postulates that he took it, along with as many other precious articles as he could, immediately after Nadir's assassination. The other says that it remained in Persia with Shah Rukh Mirza, the blind boy-king, until he presented it to Ahmad Shah in 1749. This is quite possible, for in that year Ahmad returned from Afghanistan and gave considerable aid to the shah.

Ahmad had two reasons for his return from the mountains: he wanted to include some of the richer lowlands in the infant Afghani state, and he wanted to help Shah Rukh, the only surviving descendant of both Nadir and the Savafids and, in Ahmad's eyes, the legal king. It was at that time that the upstart Arab chieftain was strutting around Khorasan; Shah Rukh was languishing in prison. Ahmad occupied Herat, then, hearing that the Arab was in Meshed, some 300 miles north-west of Herat, marched there to fight him. The Arab was killed in battle – and Meshed was taken. However, though Ahmad kept Herat, he relinquished Meshed and made Khorasan a separate state with Shah Rukh as its king. Ahmad retained suzerainty over Khurasan, yet he could have taken it entirely had he wished; he supported the blind boy simply through loyalty to Nadir's memory.

Shah Rukh certainly had a very considerable store of gems, despite his varying political fortunes, and it would have been very natural for him to have given some to Ahmad. After all, his grandfather's old general had restored his throne – even if it was over a diminished kingdom – and had guaranteed his protection. In the end it seems probable that Ahmad *was* given the jewel, and did not steal it; he and his men were fighting for their lives when they fled from the Qizilbash in Nadir's camp, and they would not have been likely to have tried to carry loot with them. It is recorded that they financed their return to the mountains, and their work there, by plundering two or three caravans on the way; and it would simply have been out of character for Ahmad to rifle his sovereign's crown jewels.

Poor Shah Rukh's time of peace lasted only until Ahmad's death. From his blindness he was a weak king, protected on one side by the unification of Afghanistan and on the other by Karim Khan's tranquil rule in Persia. But in 1773 Ahmad died, and soon afterwards another Kurdish chief captured Shah Rukh. The Kurd held Khorasan for five years, until Ahmad's son Timur restored Shah Rukh yet again; then, in the next year, 1779, Karim Khan died. In the civil strife which followed, there emerged the cruellest and most horrific character of all the Persian episodes.

Agha Mohammed Khan was an unpleasant person in every way. To look at, he was slight and wasted; a portrait of him shows a thin, morose, lined face wearing an enormous jewelled crown, spindly shoulders supporting heavily jewelled robes, the outsize garments making the mean body look even smaller. His sole loves were jewels and power; both his avarice and his cruelty became legendary. He was incapable of other loves; at the age of five he had been castrated by Ali Quli Khan, Nadir's successor, for he was the eldest son of an antagonistic and powerful tribal prince. It has been suggested that this personal disaster was the motive for all his later viciousness, but this seems superficial psychology. Evil can become a successful way of life far more easily than good; Agha Mohammed was one of those personalities whom weaker people follow for their own safety.

But not even his own people were safe from his capricious acts. One of his less disgusting habits was personally to disembowel any servant who might displease him. With this man, the use of blinding as a punishment – and as a means of making his enemies as impotent as himself – reached a kind of climax. In 1794, the city of Kerman, in south Persia, was taken by Agha Mohammed's forces. With his own hands he dug out the eyes of his last rival; and then he ordered that 20,000 pairs of eyes be brought to him from the conquered city. When they were duly delivered, heaped on trays, he counted them with the point of his dagger, saying to the officer who brought them, 'If one be missing, your own will make up the account.' But all the 40,000 eyes were there.

Two years later, after a generation of perpetual warfare, Agha Mohammed was crowned Shah of Persia. Of himself, the eunuch could not found a dynasty; however, he had a nephew. He also had one remaining fear: Shah Rukh, the blind king, still groping his way around Khorasan at the age of sixty-one. Shah Rukh had two sons, so a restoration of the Savafid dynasty was conceivable; that alone would have been enough to set Agha Mohammed on his trail. But almost as important to the avaricious eunuch were the Persian crown jewels, which Shah Rukh still possessed. Directly after his coronation, Agha Mohammed set out on the hunt.

The first quarry came easily. Shah Rukh's sons deserted him and fled to Afghanistan. Stumbling hopelessly and alone through his palace, the shah could offer no opposition. The second quarry, the jewels, were a little more difficult: Shah Rukh had hidden them all. The eunuch was not a person to hesitate at torture, and one by one the hiding-places of the gems were revealed. The process went on for several days; after each revelation Shah Rukh swore he had no more to give, but each new torture brought new treasures to light. So though the Koh-i-noor was actually in Afghanistan, Agha Mohammed remained convinced that the Shah still had it. The last gem to be disclosed was a great ruby taken by Nadir at the sack of Delhi; and to gain this, the final torture in the hunt for the crown jewels was a macabre mimicry of coronation. Shah Rukh's head was shaved, and a circle of thick paste was put around his bare scalp; then, into the circle, Agha Mohammed poured a pitcherful of molten lead.

> By blood we are immersed in love of you.
> The youth lose their heads for your sake.
> I come to you, and my heart finds rest.
> Away from you, grief clings to my heart like a snake.
> I forget the throne of Delhi
> When I remember the mountain-tops of my Pushtun land;
> If I must choose between the world and you,
> I shall not hesitate to claim your barren deserts as my own.

Ahmad Shah Abdali, sometime general in the army of Nadir Shah of Persia, originator of the Afghan state, was a poet as well. In Afghan's society where nine out of ten people, even today, are unable to read or write, there is a strong literary tradition; there are still blind poets who will recite the entire holy Qur'an, the peasants whose turn of phrase can ring like poetry in the ear, the folk who by oral tradition will speak of Omar Khayyam. In any non-literate society, the folk-tales and poetry of folklore provide a system of cohesion and an explanation of life, and Ahmad's verse above epitomizes many aspects of life in his Afghanistan.

When he returned from Persia in 1747, it was to a country ruled by many different tribes, separated by differences in terrain from desert plains to icy mountains, by innumerable varieties of local customs, by dialects and languages. There were really only two common denominators throughout the land: the religion of Islam – and in the far north even that held no sway – and everywhere a fierce, proud independence of any sovereign power.

Afghanistan then, as now, was a land of extremes with infinite shades of variation between. The physical heart of the country is the south-west end of the Hindu Kush, in geographical terms a young range – only 160 million years old or so – where the peaks rear as high as 17,000 feet, and deep dark valleys plunge between, the one sometimes completely cut off from the next. To the south-west lie extensive desert regions: stony deserts and sandy deserts; to the east, the mountains continue past Kabul and Badakhshan. North are the plains of Turkestan; south, the lower mountains and foothills of Kandahar; and west, the lowlands of Herat – the area Ahmad took from Persia in 1749.

Before then he had already made a strike at India. Many people know the name at least of the Ottoman Empire; far fewer have even heard of the Durrani Empire. Yet, at its peak, in the latter part of the eighteenth century, the Durrani were second in power in the Moslem world only to the Ottomans. To change his tribal name from Abdali to Durrani ('Pearls') was the first of many astute psychological moves which Ahmad made: it indicated an ending of old inter-tribal feuds and made other chieftains more prepared to follow. And the first line of his verse – 'By blood we are immersed in love of you' – indicates the way he organized Afghanistan. The only way other tribes could be persuaded to acknowledge Durrani leadership was by swift material gain; in no way would they accept a secondary role in the abstract creation of a nation-state. The youth would 'lose their heads' for the chance of loot, but not for love of another tribe. However, when men of other tribes followed Ahmad's promises of reward through conquest, they had to accept his discipline, and seeing their own leaders obey the Durrani, they slowly came to accept his leadership at home.

Echoing the achievements of Mahmud of Ghazni seven and a half centuries before, the Afghans under Ahmad Shah invaded India eight times. The first was in 1748; Ahmad went virtually directly from Persia to India, gathering the tribal warriors on the way. By a curious coincidence, the Mogul army which opposed them – and defeated them – was led by another Ahmad Shah, the Mogul crown prince. The two namesakes fought sporadically for another six years; the Durrani always came to India in the autumn and winter, when the southern plains were cooler and farming in the mountains was at a minimum. In January 1757, he and his men charged down for the fourth time, and occupied Delhi. Like Nadir, Ahmad left the Mogul emperor on the throne, and the Mogul – still the 'Great Mogul' – paid tribute to the Afghan. Like Nadir again, Ahmad was determined to conquer and rule; but he, too, understood the impossibility of actually taking over the subcontinent. At its peak his empire reached to Agra, but his direct rule did not extend so far; even in the Punjab, much nearer home, his conquest had to be repeated time and again. The Afghans swept through the Punjab in January 1761, this time with French mercenaries helping them; the combined force overwhelmed the Mahrattas, who had penetrated that far north. Ironically for the Afghans, their victory prepared the way for later rulers: the Sikhs and the British.

Babur and Ahmad would probably have liked each other, had they ever been able to meet. Both were mountain people, and neither felt at home in the hot plains of Hindustan; and both were of that peculiarly attractive breed, the warrior-poet. Ahmad's 'Pushtun land' was one and the same as Babur's Kabul; certainly, Babur would have found far greater affinity with the Durrani than with his own descendants in Delhi.

> Whatever countries I conquer in the world,
> I would never forget your beautiful gardens.
> When I remember the summits of your beautiful mountains,
> I forget the greatness of the Delhi throne.

Either of these poet-warrior-kings could have written the verse; in fact, it is by Ahmad. Though one could freeze in the mountains of the kingdom of Kabul, or roast in its empty deserts, the wild homeland always held their hearts. Hunting jewels and gold in India was great sport; but back home there were the groves of tamarisk, the feathery evergreen shrub with its pink and white flowers; there was hawking for partridge, pheasant and quail; there was the chase for ibex and gazelle; and there were always quarrelsome neighbouring tribes to occupy the empty hours. His mountains and deserts drew Ahmad back every time.

Now, there are four major highways traversing the nation; but Afghanistan is one of those countries which does not change much. Sometimes one may still see a group of horsemen galloping out of the desert, rifles held aloft; there are still the wandering nomads, their camel-trains lurching from one pasture to the next, the black tents springing like mushrooms against the sand and rock; still the bazaars and gardens in the cities; and still the distinctive modes of tribal dress, the various colourings of turbans, the bristling beards. The hospitality towards strangers remains; and so does the inward-looking nature of the people, and the ancient inter-tribal jealousy.

Undeniably, Ahmad united his country, fusing the feuding tribes into one army; but he never fused their minds. Though he is remembered in Afghanistan as Ahmad Shah Baba – father of his country – the very name of the country is really a foreign invention.

More accurately, it might be called Pushtunistan – 'my Pushtun land' – for the speakers of Pushtun are the majority, and have been since Ahmad's day. There are two official languages, of which Pushtun is the more widely spoken, and Dari – a modified Persian – which is the lingua franca throughout. It is also the 'court language', just as it was in Mogul Delhi. A language both expresses and creates a way of thought; the two act reciprocally, each affecting and changing the other. Ahmad's empire was essentially another one-man show, and rather than try to force his own language upon his people, he used their very differences to a constructive end. He was certainly a great man – a great leader, a great organizer and a man of vision – but greatness is not necessarily inherited, and charisma can fade. Ahmad created a Durrani empire, a tribal dominion over other tribes, but not a national consciousness. Only now is that even beginning to emerge. If the country named Afghanistan by foreigners were renamed Pushtunistan – and in the middle of the twentieth century, this became a crucial national issue – it would be a most effective denial of all the other ways of thought in this ever-various land, and once again the country would be faced with the kind of rebellion, fission and dissolution which occurred after Ahmad's death.

The reign of man on earth is short; Ahmad shortened his own reign voluntarily. Unlike his own one-time sovereign, Nadir, he did not become tyrannical, nor was he assassinated – though there were probably many men of other tribes who would have killed him. He died of a cancer that ate at his face, dissolving his nose while he lived into a maggoty hole. When he was dying, he went to the mountains near Kandahar, leaving the rule of his empire to his son Timur; and with Timur he left the Koh-i-noor.

The jewel remained with the Durranis for another forty-one years, until a new and more virile unity arose in the east; and then coming down from the cold Afghani mountains, the diamond returned to India. In Afghanistan it was owned successively by Timur and by two of his twenty-three sons, Zaman Shah and Shah Shuja. These two brothers had the distinction of each being king during the lifetime of the other; indeed, Shah Shuja was king *twice*, through no virtue of his own.

But if neither king ruled through personal virtue, it was not entirely their own fault either that they both lost their kingdom. For thousands of years Afghanistan had been a place that armies went through on their way to somewhere else. Quite suddenly, the existence of Ahmad's empire changed the old role; instead of being a series of tribes who could be fought individually, the country became a political entity able to act as a whole. As such, it was worth while for the neighbours to take it seriously; and they took it very seriously indeed.

Timur's reign lasted twenty-one years, from 1772 to 1793, and virtually his entire time was spent moving as fast as he could around the country, desperately trying to plug rebellions like a man in a leaky boat. About the time of Timur's death, Napoleon was approaching the height of his powers in Europe; the British were increasing their areas of rule in India; the Persians, somewhat recovered, were glancing covetously at Afghanistan; and the Russians were doing the same.

The situation in Afghanistan during the last quarter of the eighteenth century and the first quarter of the nineteenth was rather like a comic-book fight – a cloud of dust obscuring everything, protagonists jumping rashly in and being thrown rudely out; and, at the end, when the dust settled, finding themselves sitting dazedly opposite friends and next to enemies.

Far south in the Indian sub-continent, the English had steadily gained ground since the final expulsion of the French interest in 1752. Napoleon's European successes seemed to put any dream within his grasp, and at the turn of the century he determined to make good the French defeat. In more and more directions, India and its ordinary people were being drawn into the political and economic webs of far-distant states. Visions of imperialism occupied Britain, Tsarist Russia and Napoleonic France, and all were focused on India. The British were there already and were determined to remain; the French had been there and were determined to get back. The Russians primarily wanted the release of their enslaved countrymen in Afghanistan; and if they happened to take the country over at the same time, they would be beautifully poised for an extended holiday in India. The Persian interest was two-fold: Afghanistan was seen as a welcome possible addition to their own territory; and their country was thought to be a possible route from France to India.

In addition to this quadrilateral external pressure, the Afghans had to cope with their own nature, their love of independence. And the reaction of most 'Afghans' to the pressure was one of all-round aggression, every tribe for itself. Zaman Shah inherited the Durrani throne, for what it was worth, in 1793. In 1800 his brother Mahmud blinded him and became king; and in 1803, Shuja, brother of both, imprisoned Mahmud. Six years later Mahmud escaped and took over again.

But Mahmud never got the Koh-i-noor; Zaman took it with him into prison and buried it in the wall of his cell. An officer in the Bengal Army, one Lieutenant-Colonel W. H. Sleeman, 'received a narrative of this from Shah Zuman, the blind old king himself', and published the story in 1844 as part of his *Rambles and Recollections*. The book has a charming dedication to his sister, including this line: 'Of one thing I must beg you to be assured, that I have nowhere indulged in fiction.' Here is the relevant passage from Sleeman's book.

> He [Zaman] concealed the great diamond in a crevice in the wall of the room in which he was confined, and the rest of his jewels in a hole made in the ground with his dagger. Mahmood demanded the jewels, but Zuman Shah pretended he had thrown them into the river as he passed over. Two years after this the third brother, the Sultan Shoojah, deposed Mahmood [and] ascended the throne by the consent of

his older brother. He intended to put out the eyes of his deposed brother Mahmood but was dissuaded from it by his mother and Zuman Shah, who now pointed out to him the place where he had concealed the great diamond.

It is worth mentioning that Zaman's account, transmitted through Sleeman, does not say that Ahmad stole the jewel from Nadir's camp. Neither does it say that Shah Rukh presented the stone to Ahmad. According to Zaman, Ahmad 'took the diamond from Shah Rukh, since it could be of no use to a man who could no longer see its beauties'. Bearing Ahmad's loyalty to Nadir in mind, it seems doubtful whether he would have stolen it from the shepherd-king's grandson; the most probable explanation is that Shah Rukh offered him the choice of his jewels.

In Afghanistan it was not only brother against brother; half-brother against half-brother, cousin against cousin, tribe against tribe – everyone fought; and behind it all the other nations played their games of power. Full civil war took Afghanistan in 1819 and held it for seven years; and then, in 1826, a very distant cousin of the Durranis appeared, and disposed of them all for a while. His name was Dost Mohammed; 'Dost' means friend.

In 1836, an Englishman named Vigne decided to visit Kabul. He was one of many Britons who wandered around India at that time, an odd collection of very individual characters who were prepared to go anywhere by any means; some journeyed for commercial reasons, some for political motives. Many went travelling through the new British dominions and beyond simply through curiosity, which was Vigne's motive.

When the idea of visiting Kabul occurred to him, he happened to be staying at Ludhiana; so he was able to meet two other people who were staying there at the same time.

> I was introduced by Captain Wade to Shah Shuja and Zaman Shah, the pensioned ex-kings of the country I was going to visit . . . Shah Zaman sat on the ground, pale, thin, dejected, and counting his beads. He asked much about Kashmir, and said that the shawls were not now so fine as they used to be. 'I remember', he said, 'when the finer fabrics could be drawn through a ring.' He was praising the beauty of Kashmir. 'Yes', said the poor blind monarch, 'Kashmir is certainly beautiful, and the water and air are good; but,' he continued with a melancholy shake of the head, and a sigh as deep as ever I

heard, 'Kabul, Kabul! What is Kashmir to Kabul? And I shall never see it again!'

It was the same agony of exile that Ahmad and Babur had known. Shuja and Zaman were not on good terms – not surprisingly – and Shuja lived in another part of the building.

'We found Shah Shuja sitting on a chair in a recess, or rather doorway, of his house, with a vista, formed by two rows of attendants, that diverged from it as from a centre.' The Shah, who was wearing a dark robe, a white turban and white cotton gloves, was 'about fifty; of the middle size, good-natured, and port-wine complexioned, looking more like a country gentlemen who had lost an estate than a monarch who had lost a kingdom'.

The fact was that the phlegmatic shah was quite enjoying his exile and the freedom from the responsibility of rule. 'The next morning,' Vigne noted, 'Shah Shuja sent us several trays, containing the best display of native cookery I had seen in the East; it had probably been superintended in management by the ladies of the harem.' But Shuja had not only lost the Durrani empire, he had also lost the Durrani diamond. By the time that he and Vigne met, the Koh-i-noor had found a new owner; and yet the jewel was not far away. It was in Lahore, about 120 miles from the two exiled Afghans.

Six

The Lion and All His Cubs

The Sikhs – Ranjit Singh, the 'Lion of the Punjab' – his rapid rise to being Rajah of the Punjab – events in India since Nadir Shah – the growth of British power in India – Ranjit's character – his children, real and claimed – Francophobia in India – incident at Amritsar – Ranjit and the British – Ranjit's acquisition of the Koh-i-noor – his way of life – his death and bequest of the diamond to a temple

By the nineteenth century, everyone knew that the Sikhs were exceptionally good fighters. A Sikh is not a man of a particular race, but of a particular religion. Sikhism is a mixture of Hinduism, Islam and Buddhism, an eclectic faith comparable to Akbar's Din-i-Illahi. It started near Lahore, around the beginning of the sixteenth century. In a manner slightly reminiscent of Buddhism, it was an attempt to return to the original purity of Hindu ideas, as they were before they vanished under layers of gods and myths and idols. This, at any rate, was the intention of the first of the ten Sikh gurus, Guru Nanak, who died in 1538. For well over 100 years after his death it continued as just that, one of the innumerable small and virtually anonymous sects in the vast bulk of Hinduism. Then, in 1675, something happened which was to change Sikhism, and India, permanently: Aurangzeb, in one of his religious wars against the Hindus, tortured a Sikh to death for his religion. The martyr's son Govind escaped to the mountains – the boy was fifteen at the time. Fifteen years later, he emerged as the tenth and last guru of the Sikhs, and he gave them a new code to live by. It was a warriors' code, and it was suffused with a terrrible hatred of Islam and the Moslems.

Nanak had been a teacher of ethics; Govind was a teacher of politics. But Govind did not try to change or overthrow Nanak's words; he simply provided a channel for the Sikhs' martial energy. After the time of Guru Govind the faith became more and more militant. A Hindu is born but not made; it is the opposite with a Sikh. A child is not born into the faith but joins it – or does not – when he is old enough to decide for himself. The *pahul,* the baptism of a Sikh, is a vivid little sketch of Sikh life. It began with Nanak, fell into disuse and then was revived by Govind. The ceremony begins with a piece of sugar-candy being dissolved in water; the water must be pure, and the sugar is dissolved by being stirred with a dagger. At the same time verses from the *Granth*, the Sikh holy book, are recited over it. The person to be baptized drinks some of the water; the remainder is sprinkled over him, and he shouts, *Guruji ka khalsa!* – 'Victory to the *khalsa* of the guru'. In time the *khalsa* became specifically the Sikh army, but at that stage it signified the whole of Sikhdom, the Sikh commonwealth; and like much of the Sikh way of life, the little ceremony that makes a person a member of the *khalsa* is simple, practical and to the point. After his baptism, a new Sikh can add the name 'Singh' to his birth-name. It means lion.

The new Sikh will also wear five distinctive emblems. Five is a powerful number in Sikh mythology, and the Punjabi names of all the five things begin with K. They are *kes,* uncut hair and beard – the thick hair, closely wrapped inside a turban, could help deflect a sword-blow; then *khanda,* the dagger; *kanga,* a wooden comb; *kara,* an iron bangle worn round the wrist as a symbol of virility; and lastly *kuchh,* that is, a pair of short knee-length drawers. This last made a very obvious visual distinction between the Sikh and the ordinary Hindu, always clad in his loin-cloth, or *dhoti*.

Guru Govind Singh took his followers to war soon, against some Rajputs. Aurangzeb sent reinforcements to the Rajputs. In an early battle, Govind's two eldest sons were killed by the Rajputs; then his two younger ones were captured, and Aurangzeb ordered them to be buried alive.

Govind was the last of the Sikh gurus. In many ways he was the most important, for he gave them the distinct military stamp they have retained ever since. After his death in 1708 – the year after Aurangzeb – he was succeeded by a military leader called Banda, and for a few years the proud, ambitious *khalsa* operated successfully against the imperial forces; then in 1716 Banda and several thousand other Sikhs were defeated and tortured to death in Delhi. For a generation thereafter the Sikhs in the Punjab kept very quiet indeed.

Then Nadir Shah came through and showed that Delhi was not omnipotent; the Sikh spirits revived at the terrible thought of Moslems walking over their country, and with considerable verve began to fight every Moslem they could – Moguls, Persians and Afghans too, for by that time Ahmad Shah and his men were beginning to stalk across the Punjab.

Now one of the basic features of the Sikh way of life was the idea of brotherhood and equality, and it was possible for this to be realized to some extent when the Sikhs were united against the Moslems. In actual numbers the Sikhs were always far in the minority, not only through India as a whole but even in the Punjab. No censuses were taken before 1855, but throughout the latter half of the nineteenth century the ratio of Sikhs to other souls was usually about one to twelve, and one might reasonably suppose that the Sikh could have an unending supply of infidels to destroy. But, in general, army service was seasonal, for men must grow and gather food, and in peacetime the Sikhs were farmers. And because they were farmers, they led fairly sedentary lives. They had their land and they liked it, and they did not see much reason to move. In short, unless the Moslems actually came through their territory, the Sikhs did not usually go out after them – and if there were no Moslems about, they would fight each other. This obviously did not spring from any strong sense of brotherhood, but in an odd way it did come from the equality, for no Sikh – except in admiration or in final self-defence – would take another as his leader. However, among these strong characters, one emerged who was stronger than all the rest.

Ranjit Singh certainly did not look like a story-book hero. He was a small man, blind in one eye and with his face badly pitted from smallpox, and everyone who met him said he was very ugly. And yet everyone said as well that there was something almost magical about him, something that made one instinctively obey him, something that took away the power to disobey. This quality stayed with him all his life; in his last years, he became partly paralysed, dumb and very feeble, but British visitors would still comment with awe on his complete control of his court and country.

He had had an early start; in 1791, when his father died, Ranjit was only eleven, and heir to a powerful chieftaincy. He took full power as chieftain when he was seventeen, and then, in a completely characteristic manner, started to acquire new land. Zaman, the Afghan king, was still king at this time and not yet blind, and he made several invasions of the Punjab. From Zaman's view, none of these had a lasting effect, for the Sikhs would vanish when he arrived and would return after he had left. Ahmad Shah had created such a legend for tough fighting around his Afghan warriors that not even the martial Sikhs wanted to face them.

Ranjit used Zaman's invasions as levers for his own advancement. While a region was disorganized, immediately following one of Zaman's trips, Ranjit would move into it and take it over. Zaman even occupied Lahore, the capital of the Punjab, in 1797. He had to move out in the spring of 1798, to patch up Afghanistan; and by the summer Ranjit had moved in. This time, however, some of the other Sikhs thought he was going too far, first, because Lahore was the Punjabi capital, and secondly, because Ranjit had been given a formal grant to Lahore by Zaman, the invader himself.

So four other tribes joined together to oust him, and marched towards Lahore with a large army. About twenty-five miles short of Lahore they stopped, facing Ranjit's army; and there everyone sat for two months. Ranjit did not seem very perturbed; he probably knew that two of the four tribes were members of the Bhangi confederation. *Bhang* means hashish, and the Bhangi were so named because they used the drug in great quantities; and while Ranjit sat and patiently did nothing, the opposing force began to have a tremendous party, going on all of every night and most of every day. The convivial atmosphere lasted for several weeks, until all of a sudden one of the Bhangi chiefs had a fit of *delirium tremens* and died. The rest sobered up rapidly, and with great speed decided to go home. Ranjit was left master of Lahore. He never lost it.

And thus, by his eighteenth year, this most extraordinary young man – already blind in one eye – had made himself Rajah of Lahore and ruler of a large proportion of the Punjab, and was gathering all the trappings of sovereignty around himself. In the year 1800, when he was twenty, he declared himself Maharaja – 'Great King', a monarch to whom other monarchs were tributary vassals – and from then on, events in his life moved faster and faster. He did not have an exceptionally long life – he died when he was fifty-nine – but he lived very hard indeed, and before he was fifty everyone spoke of him as the old king.

Indeed, at fifty he looked much older than most people do at seventy: his tiny body partly wasted by paralysis; his skin pocked, his one eye constantly moving, his beard very long and white, his hands nervously holding a visitor's for half an hour at a time. He had the misfortune, too, to be one of the people remembered mostly from paintings done when he was old. Those people seem always to have been old; and yet Ranjit, even if he never cut a very dashing figure of physical strength, achieved a large part of his life's work while still a very young man.

But, in order to clarify all the events of the next busy few years, we should look briefly at events in India since Nadir's sack of Delhi.

It had really been a continuous round-robin of war and battle, involving French, Mahratta and Mogul forces. In the 1740s, the French had come close to winning the first steps towards an Indian empire, and two Anglo-French wars had ensued. There had been the battles of Arcot and Trichinopoly, when Robert Clive began the process of making himself a living legend; in 1756 the Durrani, Ahmad Shah, had occupied Delhi, and in the following year the battle of Plassey had taken place. That battle had had immediate important political effects – its first result being that the East India Company became landlord of 900 square miles of India. And then, for a while, the 'dual system' of rule existed, in which the traditional Indian ministers continued to act their parts while power actually rested in British hands. This came to an end in 1772, when Warren Hastings became Governor of Bengal with orders from the company to rule directly, without a puppet in front of him.

The French had been knocked out of the running in 1752, and during the entire period the Moguls had been growing less and less significant, so the contest began to run between the British and the Mahrattas. In 1772, the Mahratta Confederacy was the largest political unit in India, occupying about a third of the subcontinent. Indeed, from 1788 to 1803 they even occupied Delhi; but at the turn of the century there was one more shift in the balance, and this time it was going to last. Lord Wellesley, brother of the Duke of Wellington, became governor-general in 1798. He arrived in India intending to create an empire; and within six years the company controlled most of the south, all of the eastern coast, part of the western coast, all of Bengal and most of the north-eastern border through to the Punjab. In short, by the beginning of the nineteenth century, the British were the dominant power in India; and the Sikhs had to come to terms with this.

At the same time as Lord Wellesley was annexing large areas in the south, Ranjit, the Lion of the Punjab, was busily extending his own dominions by conquest, annexation, treachery and threat. Often, after having overrun some small principality, he would leave its previous ruler in charge as before, simply requiring an oath of loyalty and an annual tribute from the conquered man. Often, too, as his reputation increased, he found that there was no need to fight; he would arrive in yet another small state to find that his fame, or notoriety, had preceded him, and the state's ruler was already waiting to surrender.

In such cases he accepted the offered victory and soon moved on. And this shows an important difference between the type of man that Ranjit was and the types represented by Nadir, or Aurangzeb, or the Persian eunuch-king Agha Mohammed. Nadir fought because he liked fighting; conquest was almost a secondary thing, an outcome of successful fighting. Aurangzeb fought because he believed deeply in the truth of his own religion and none other; with him, too, the extension of empire was of rather lesser importance. Both Nadir and Aurangzeb became tyrannical and cruel towards their foes; Agha Mohammed was simply and horribly sadistic. In sharp contrast, Ranjit's first objective was conquest, but conquest of a limited and specific nature: he wanted to unify the *khalsa*. And though, obviously, people died because of him, he did not indulge in gratuitous cruelty and torture. He was not a religious bigot, either – in that, as in almost everything else, he followed his own counsel. It was typical of the man that when he fell in love, at twenty-two years old, with an outstandingly beautiful girl, he went ahead and married her, despite the fact that she was an accursed Moslem. He was as illiterate as he was self-willed, and once began a heated discussion on the name 'Shalamar'; he had decided that the name meant 'God's Curse', which seemed to him an odd name for a garden. He made the derivation from the Hindu word *'mar'*, meaning 'a curse', and a dialect word *'shala,'*, meaning 'god'. And he completely refused to believe his courtiers' explanation that both words were Turkish, that *Shala* meant 'pleasure' and *mar* meant 'place'; so he renamed it Shala Bagh. This time the words are Persian – *shala* is 'sweetheart', *bagh* is 'garden'. Not one of the courtiers dared gainsay him; but then, his idea was not so far from the original.

In 1805, when Wellesley's annexations were at their peak, the three powers – British, Sikh and Mahratta – became mutually involved for the first time. A Mahratta leader named Holkar was being chased with his men by an English army, and the hunt was headed directly for the Punjab. Holkar hoped to find refuge and support with Ranjit, but the Sikh saw no reason to allow two other nations to use his infant state as a battleground. Various minor Sikh chiefs further south had aided Holkar in vain; Ranjit probably would have commented that giving such aid indicated why they were only minor chiefs. He was committed to creating a united republic based around the *khalsa*, and needed all his strength to raise his cubs. But he did act as a mediator between the Mahrattas and the British, and they managed to reach a peaceful agreement; this left him unharmed and friends with both – a typically astute move.

Ranjit had one cub of his own, his son and heir-apparent, Kharak, born in 1802. Connected with his several wives he also had a number of scheming mothers-in-law, and in 1807 one of these announced that her daughter was pregnant. The lady in question had not conceived any children before, and her reputed pregnancy was conveniently made to last throughout one of Ranjit's sessions of conquest in the surrounding countryside. When he returned he was presented with two bouncing new-born sons. He liked them well enough, and they were given princely names and titles; but he knew all along that they were not his. One was the son of a chintz-weaver, the other the son of a slave; both had been bought on the day of their birth.

Many years later, in 1835, a similar thing happened when a dancing-girl, whom Ranjit had found attractive, produced a son. The true father was a water-carrier, but the girl, sensing the chance of a better future for her boy, maintained that he was Ranjit's child. The Maharaja was well into middle age by that time, and had had a stroke, but he accepted the child. The baby boy was named Dhulip.

Those early years of the century saw one other very important development in the unification of the Sikhs: the downfall of Afghanistan. In 1798 Zaman and the very name of Afghan were sources of fear and respect for the Sikhs. Only five years later, when their game of musical thrones was well under way, the entire Afghan nation had become contemptible, and Ranjit began extending his power into the lands east of the Indus, which hitherto had been exclusively Afghani.

Another name for the Punjab is the Land of the Five Rivers. Of the five, the Indus, flowing south-west through Sind to the Indian Ocean, is the largest and most important; the others are all tributaries of the Indus. They are the Jhelum, the Chenab, the Ravi and the Sutlej. Further south, and flowing south, lies the Jumna – the river which runs beside Delhi and Agra and beside which Babur made his 'Kabul' garden. There were Sikh tribes throughout this area, from the Indus to the banks of the Jumna, and when Ranjit took to calling himself Lord of all the Khalsa, it became apparent that he intended to control the lot. Unfortunately for him, there were a good many Sikhs who had no wish to come under his control; and so in 1808 a new phase began, and the Sikhs and the British had to acknowledge each other.

It began in March 1808 with the Cis-Sutlej tribes, the Sikhs on the south bank of the Sutlej. They simply did not want to be conquered, and they sent a deputation to Delhi asking for British help. The British refused. Then all of a sudden everyone did an about-face: Ranjit began to make conciliatory noises, the Cis-Sutlej chiefs decided to trust to luck with him, and the British began sending envoys to *him* asking for help. It was the period of Francophobia, when every Briton in India awoke each morning expecting Bonaparte to come marching towards the sub-continent. Embassies were sent not only to Ranjit, but also to the Persian and Afghan courts; all of them could be effective barriers against land attack.

Ranjit thought it a lot of nonsense. He simply did not believe it was possible for a French army to come overland, across thousands of miles of mountain and desert, and of course he was perfectly right. It seemed to him that the British were up to some sort of trickery which he could not fathom, and so he decided to ignore them and carry on subduing the Cis-Sutlej. It was partly through pique that the British then decided to protect the Cis-Sutlej from him, and shortly afterwards the illiterate Lion of the Punjab received a strong letter. He prepared for war.

In fact, Ranjit and the British never went to war. Not only that, but within a few months of the Lion's first bellicose preparations, the two sides had become good friends; and they remained so all of Ranjit's life. This happened almost unintentionally; it was Ranjit's idiosyncratic reaction to an incident at Amritsar, in January 1809.

The Moslem religious festival of Muharram came at that time, and among the escort of the British Envoy to Ranjit there were a fair number of faithful Moslems. The fact that they were in Amritsar, a Sikh city, did nothing to put the Moslems off their celebrations, and they went ahead with considerable style. The Moslems, as usual, made models of various sacred tombs, and as usual, these were carried in procession around the city, with bands playing and the assembled company singing. It was really a very brave thing to do, since the Moslems could scarcely have forgotten the deep enmity borne to them by the Sikhs. To a conscientious Sikh, it was an extremely provocative action. Ranjit probably did not care twopence, seeing that he had married a Moslem girl; but some people did care. There was one group in particular called the Akali, the 'Immortals'; and these were the fanatics of Sikhdom. As the procession came past their buildings, the Akali opened fire against this flagrant insult to their religion and their holy city. The model tombs were shot to pieces, and the Moslems reacted immediately to the insult to *their* religion. Battle was joined, with the Sikhs heavily outnumbering the Moslems. But it was not fought as a simple street brawl; the Moslems had been trained as British soldiers, and from habit and assurance fought as such. The consequence was that the Sikhs, fighting in a totally disorganized manner, were soundly beaten.

Ranjit was very impressed. He realized that if he went to war against the British for the Cis-Sutlej states and the complete unity of the *khalsa*, he had a good chance of losing everything; and so he stopped arguing. That one incident had been more expressive than any plea or threat; the Lion's cubs withdrew to the north of the Sutlej, and a treaty of friendship was drawn up between Ranjit and the British.

In Afghanistan, the embassy seeking union against the French had been successful in a more straightforward way. The monarch of the day was the amiable and ineffective Shah Shuja. He had been quite happy to sign a treaty with the British against the imagined threat of the French; he was a cautious man, and it seems likely that a major consideration in his decision was the idea that British soldiers would protect *him* against the French.

Mountstuart Elphinstone, the British envoy, was nearly overcome by the shah's clothes:

> We thought at first that he had on an armour of jewels; but on close inspection, we found this to be a mistake, and his real dress to consist of a green tunic, with large flowers worked in gold and precious stones, over which were a large breast-plate of diamonds, shaped like two flattened fleurs-de-lys, an ornament of the same kind on each thigh, large emerald bracelets on the arms (above the elbows), and many other jewels in many places. In one of these bracelets was the Koh-i-noor, known to be one of the largest diamonds in the world.

But despite the splendour of his outfit, Shuja was dethroned almost before the ink on the treaty was dry. The king had not even been able to meet the envoy in the Afghan capital, the disturbances in the country were so great; Elphinstone did not go further than Peshawar, and he had to return very quickly. Yet quick as he was, he was overtaken while passing through Sikh territory by the blind Shah Zaman and Shuja's fugitive harem.

Shuja was really a very pathetic figure. He enjoyed being a king, and in a more peaceful country than Afghanistan he might have been quite good at it. As it was, he was simply too soft for such a tough, recalcitrant people. The will for independence still ran strongly in Afghani veins, and when tribes revolted, Shuja would forgive their leaders and ask them not to do it again. Some appreciated this; even after he was thrown out in 1809, he still had a respectable number of followers. He fought a series of losing battles for a few years, vainly trying to regain the kingdom; then, in 1812, he was captured, and imprisoned in Kashmir.

It is not known when or how Ranjit first heard of the Koh-i-noor; quite probably he had known of it all his life, for it was certainly sufficiently famous. Among his other contradictory qualities, the Lion of the Punjab was both immensely generous and extremely greedy. He loved to gain and to give enormous quantities of money, jewels and goods of all descriptions. In particular, he loved jewels, so when Zaman turned up in Lahore in despair at Shuja's capture, it must have seemed to Ranjit a truly god-given chance.

The one-eyed maharaja comforted the blind ex-king, and his family, and Shuja's family – all of whom had come for refuge at Lahore – and tugged his beard with a suitably pensive air. And then (no doubt choosing his moment carefully) he said it might be possible to rescue Shuja. But Ranjit had his price, and his price was the diamond.

Shuja's wife agreed on her husband's behalf. In due course Kashmir was attacked; the shah was freed and brought to Lahore by the triumphant Sikhs. The rescue operation was conducted in a way quite typical of Ranjit's military opportunism: an army belonging to the new Afghan king was advancing on Kashmir at exactly the same time as Ranjit's force. The two armies met, and their leaders agreed to make the reduction of Kashmir a joint project, out of which Ranjit would take a third of the loot. It was winter, and bitterly cold. The Afghans, accustomed to the mountains, made light of it, but the Sikhs suffered badly; and when they all eventually arrived in Kashmir, the Sikhs were unable to do much fighting. Had they been alone, they could not have won; as it was, they were able to sit back and recover while the Afghans did the dirty work. And thus, quite unintentionally, the ex-king of Afghanistan was freed by the army of the new king, his own rebellious brother.

Ranjit never got his third of the spoil, which angered him considerably – even though he had done little to earn it – but he did get the king, and he meant to get the diamond. Unfortunately, it was not quite as easy as he expected. Shah Shuja had known nothing of the agreement, supposing his rescue to have been prompted by the goodness of Ranjit's heart, and he had no wish to give up the jewel. He said he did not have it with him; his wife improved on the story, and told Ranjit her husband had pawned it in Kabul to finance his battles. It sounded a thin tale to Ranjit, and he promptly put Shuja and his dependants under house arrest. He then offered the ex-king a large sum of money and a tract of land for his maintenance in exchange for the gem. When that produced no result, Ranjit cut off food supplies to the shah for two days. Then he accused Shuja of plotting against him with other Afghans, and threatened to separate the shah from his family if he did not give up the stone at once. Shuja dithered and protested for some while longer, and then gave up.

The jewel was actually transferred on 1 June 1813, in as tardy and unwilling an atmosphere as the rest of the temperamental courtship. Shuja announced he was ready to give up the jewel, and Ranjit immediately rushed around to his apartments. There the customary greetings took place, and then the two kings sat facing each other for an hour in silence. At last Ranjit's patience gave out, and he demanded the stone; Shuja, with a sigh, produced a small roll of cloth; Ranjit unwrapped it, chortled with glee, and left without another word. Later he sent a message to Shuja saying that the jewel was fit only to grace a monarch, and since the shah no longer had a kingdom, the gem now had a far better home.

Ranjit became intensely proud of his new possession. The way he had acquired it gave him rather a bad name for a while; Sikh historians still often adopt a critical and rather shamefaced attitude when they tell the tale. Yet no shame is, or was, necessary for the Sikhs; it was a matter of honour, of promises made, kept and broken. Ranjit had kept his word and freed Shuja; when the bargain was not fulfilled immediately, the maharaja was remarkably restrained. A good many other monarchs would have cut somebody's head off instantly; but in all his time as king and conqueror, Ranjit never killed or tortured anyone in cold blood.

He tried the jewel in various different settings; Shuja, for a time, had had it surrounded with emeralds, then mounted in gold. Ranjit first tried it as a bracelet, then wore it on his turban. From that it went to decorate his horse's bridle – on the right side, so that the maharaja could see it – and then at last he returned to the first notion. The great diamond was set between two smaller ones, and the Lion wore them around his arm.

For many years few Europeans had seen the gem, but in the summer of 1838 a rather unusual group arrived for diplomatic talks with the maharaja. The group included William Osborne, who was military secretary to Lord Auckland, the governor-general. Osborne met Ranjit for the first time on 29 May; the Englishman found the Lion's court a memorable place.

> The coup d'oeil [he wrote] was most striking: every walk in the garden was lined with troops, and the whole space behind the throne was crowded with Runjeet's chiefs, mingled with natives from Candahar, Caubul and Afghanistan, blazing with gold and jewels, and dressed and armed in every conceivable variety of colour and fashion.
>
> Cross-legged in a golden chair, dressed in simple white, wearing no ornaments but a single string of enormous pearls around the waist, and the celebrated Koh-i-noor, or Mountain of Light, on his arm – (the jewel rivalled, if not surpassed, in brilliancy by the glance of fire which every now and then shot from his single eye as it wandered restlessly around the circle) – sat the Lion of Lahore.

Negotiations went on for six weeks – or to be more exact, Osborne stayed for six weeks, and every now and then the old Lion and his English visitor talked politics. There was plenty of time for reviews of Ranjit's immaculately drilled soldiers – he had taken the lesson at Amritsar closely to heart, and had engaged European generals to train his troops. There was plenty of time, too, for Ranjit's stupendously drunken parties. He had a special brandy made for his exclusive use, and for a guest to be given it was a sign of honour. The mischievous old man especially delighted to give it to Europeans, to test their staying power; the mixture was based on raisins and fortified with musk, the juices of various meats, and ground pearls. It was like liquid fire – literally, for it burnt the lips of another visitor. The unlikely potion was brewed for Ranjit by a Hungarian homeopathist named Honigberger, who also mixed the Lion's gunpowder. Perhaps the Hungarian had confused the two recipes.

Ranjit seemed to thrive on the stuff. Osborne managed to stay the course for the whole six weeks, and at the end the maharaja gave him a mark of very special favour: he let Osborne handle the Koh-i-noor.

> It certainly is a most magnificent diamond [the Englishman wrote in wonder]. It is about an inch and a half in length and upwards of an inch in width, and stands out from the setting about half an inch: it is in the shape of an egg, and is set in a bracelet between two very handsome diamonds about half its size. It is valued at three million sterling, and without a flaw of any kind.

It occurred to him briefly that few people ever held such a fortune in their hands; but before the purity of the jewel, such gross thoughts vanished; one could only gaze at it in awe and wonder.

Shuja predicted that Ranjit Singh would lose the diamond, as had he and so many others, through force. He was wrong; the Lion of the Punjab retained it all his life, and passed it on to the only son he knew to be his own.

In 1834, a few years before Osborne's visit, Ranjit had had a stroke; and a few months after the visit, the old Lion had a second stroke. It came immediately after a month's roistering in celebration of a visit by the governor-general, Lord Auckland. Ranjit had once employed an English doctor, but during his illnesses he relied on Indian medicine – perhaps because the English doctor was called Murray. For, by an odd coincidence, 'murray' was the exact nineteenth-century English transliteration of the Hindu word for a corpse.

After the second stroke, Ranjit's health declined steadily. He was partly paralysed, and could not speak. All kinds of remedies were tried, of which the favourite was the administration of powdered gems (as the only fit medicine for such a monarch). This did not work; and at last the maharaja resorted to divine propitiation. He gave away tens of thousands of rupees to the poor; he gave precious stones and great quantities of other goods, including 200 tons of cooking fat, to temples and holy men. Still it did not work. On 12 July 1839, Osborne wrote a last note in his journal.

> Runjeet Singh is dead, poor fellow! and died (on the 27th June, 1839) as like the old Lion as he had lived. He preserved his senses to the last, and was (which is unusual with native princes) obeyed to the last by all his chiefs – though he tried them hard, as you will think, when I tell you that two hours before he died, he sent for all his jewels, and gave the famous diamond, called the Mountain of Light, said to be the largest in the world, to a Hindoo temple.

However, Osborne was not quite right. Many *jewels* were given away, and the Brahmin priests, sensing a windfall, encouraged the dying man. Without a doubt life and vigour would return, they said, if only he should give away his greatest single possession. They certainly wanted the Koh-i-noor, and they almost got it; the dumb, paralysed monarch made a sign that was interpreted as assent. But then one man stepped in and prevented it, and made himself a place in history. His name was Misr Beli Ram, and he was the guardian of the *toshakhana,* the jewel-house.

Beli Ram would not let the Koh-i-noor be given in alms. In this he was not directly disobeying Ranjit – no one had ever done that; he knew how enfeebled his king was, and he did not believe that the maharaja truly wished to give the gem to the priests of Jagannath. He came to see the dying king personally, to receive his wishes at first hand, and to express his own concern.

In one way, this man, who appears and vanishes all in a moment, is the most remarkable person in the entire history of the Koh-i-noor; he wanted to protect the jewel, not for personal greed or glory, like almost everyone else, but for the sake of a principle. He explained his caution to Ranjit with an abstract concept that harked back to the ancient ideal of the *chakravartin,* the Universal Emperor: the jewel was not a personal possession, to be given away on a whim; it belonged to *the crown – not to the monarch.*

Whether Ranjit understood, whether he listened, whether he even cared by that time, is not known; but the jewel remained with the crown, and the priests had to be content.

Seven

Swallowed Up Whole

Shuja's escape from Lahore – his bids to regain the Afghan throne – the Edens in India – the First Afghan War – the Sikh uprising – the battle of Multan – Private Waterfield – the battle of Gujerat – Dalhousie and the annexation of the Punjab

Some time after handing over the Koh-i-noor to Ranjit, Shah Shuja performed the one act of his life that may be called completely successful: he escaped from Lahore. Ranjit's greed had been awakened by the great diamond and he pressed for more of the Durrani treasures, until at last even the passive Shuja had had enough. First he contrived the escape of his harem – 600 women – by the simple expedient of disguising them as ordinary Hindu women and bribing their guards. The women were taken by bullock cart to Ludhiana in British India, where they were given asylum. Shuja's own escape was somewhat more difficult, for Ranjit placed an extra guard around him, until the ex-king was surrounded by 4,000 soldiers. But bribery won through again, and one of the 4,000 gave Shuja tools to dig his way out. Shuja disguised himself as a fakir, disguised one of his servants as himself, then slipped out late one night in April 1815. He got out of the town by squelching a slippery way through the town drain under the walls, and emerged with great relief at about two in the morning. A swim across the near-by river cleaned his clothes; prayers at a saint's tomb cleaned his spirit. Then, with the dawn, he bought an ox and cart, and set off in great good temper. It is easy to imagine him trundling along in the gathering light, elated at freedom and congratulating himself. He had given 4,000 guards the slip – and he had dodged out from under the very nose of the Lion of Lahore – surely it was clear that he was set for a special fate. The triumphal mood prompted him to try and get his throne yet again; but if the mood continued, the luck did not. The one success of his life was over. His attempt for the throne was a wretched failure, and in September 1816 he joined his vast family in Ludhiana. It was there that Vigne met him nineteen years later.

*

Through those long years of exile, the dream of a reunited Durrani empire stayed with Shuja. Though he was naïve and incompetent, he was also persistent, and he made two more efforts on his own account to recover the lost empire. To finance the first, in 1832, he courted the most unlikely ally – his old captor, Ranjit Singh. The shah proposed that he should renounce all claim to the Durrani lands conquered by Ranjit, and should also finally renounce the Koh-i-noor; in return, Ranjit would supply him with men and money for the reclamation of Kabul. Secure in his possession of both lands and the jewels, it is hardly likely that Ranjit took the suggestions at all seriously.

By that time, however, the fractious Afghan tribes were getting bored with their current king, who happened to be Shuja's nephew. This young man, as inept as his uncle, had made the mistake of executing a particularly influential chieftain, whose family naturally retaliated, and having disposed of the king rather unexpectedly asked Shuja back. He set off instantly, seeing himself as a rightful monarch returning to his remorseful people, and expecting to encounter scenes of rejoicing and regret tempered with his regal mercy. Nothing could have been further from the Afghan mind, though, and he had gone no further than Peshawar when the fickle reality of the mountain people rejected him again. In all his attempts at royal power, his fatal weakness was that he never had the slightest notion of how his people really felt and thought. At Peshawar, for example, he began wearing an air of righteous indignation coupled with a magnanimity that the Afghans found most distasteful. Had he understood the popular mood more accurately, he might have been granted his throne again; as it was, he found himself back in Ludhiana almost as fast as he had left it.

Nothing daunted, the shah tried once more in 1833; and this time he appeared to be winning for a while. For nearly a year he made a leisurely progress in the general direction of Afghanistan, and all along the way he picked up large sums of money, as well as horses and guns, from local chieftains professing loyalty to the Durranis. Soon things were looking sufficiently serious for Ranjit himself to send the shah guns and money; and now the maharaja took up the previous suggestion that Shuja should renounce any claim to conquered lands and captured jewels. The wave of apparent success continued: Shuja fought and won a battle in Sind, then went on to Kandahar for the final confrontation. He should have won – he had gathered a strong army, a lot of money and a good supply of stores; and for once the people of Kabul were actually in favour of him. He did not win simply because, in the battle at Kandahar, he lost his nerve and fled. The obvious comment, and the one most usually made, was that in time of crisis Shuja was a coward. Another *possible* and at least more charitable view is this: that to come to the point of actually realizing a dream, after years of hope, can be difficult; the dream has become a way of life. Shuja may simply have been overwhelmed by the real possibility of empire.

And so, for the third time, he took refuge in Ludhiana. On each occasion, retreating with confusion and wounded pride in 1832, or fleeing in 1834, the poor man was really doing nothing more than showing that final flaw that had ended every empire the world had ever seen. The flaw, the crack in the kingdom's unity, was the loss of understanding between rulers and ruled. It was a progressive weakness, beginning when the inheritors of a ruling class claimed the right to rule without having the ability; or when privilege was claimed, and duty – – which allows privilege – was rejected. The Moguls had become pretentious puppets; Nadir, mad and tyrannical; the Durranis, honest but incompetent.

The East India Company had won privilege, and reluctantly they had accepted the accompanying duty, the responsibility of ruling. Then, having the ability, they had claimed the right to rule over constantly expanding areas of India; and over the next few years, out of a mess of intrigue, apprehension and war, the last of the Indian empires would emerge. And with the last imperial unity, the Koh-i-noor would move for the last time.

British rule of India had been inevitable since Ranjit accepted the Sutlej river as his southern boundary. Had he persisted in the Cis-Sutlej states, he might have won them. If he had, he and the British would have been relatively equal in the balance of power, for a while at least. But it was a risk he was unwilling to take; not only had he witnessed the effectiveness of the British army at Amritsar, but there were also enough tribes of dubious loyalty in the Punjab to make him wary of leaving the state for long. He preferred to trust the British, and they trusted him.

After the French scare in the early years of the century, a new phantom had arisen. In 1826, Russia and Persia had fought, and Russia had won; and ever since, Englishmen in India had lived in fear of a Russian invasion. In fact, such a thing was as remote a possibility as the feared French invasion had been, but it was a powerful nightmare; administrators and statesmen who otherwise behaved in a fairly sensible manner began to do totally absurd things. One of these was the decision to put the pathetic Shuja back on his throne again – whether he liked it or not this time – and this had been the reason for the diplomatic missions of Osborne and Auckland to the old Lion of Lahore. The theory was that a friendly Afghanistan would act as a buffer before the supposed Russian advance. However, though the current ruler of Afghanistan, Dost Mohammed, was manifestly more capable than any Durrani, and wanted British friendship, the British remained aloof from him. The trouble was that the Dost, as a condition of alliance, wanted the British to get Peshawar back for him from Ranjit, and the British were not prepared to break with their old ally in Lahore. Out of this web, in the last months of Ranjit's life, came a triple alliance: Shuja, Ranjit and the British against Dost Mohammed.

The situation was well described in 1838 by an English visitor to India: 'Whenever we want to frighten any of the neighbours into good conduct, we have one sure resource: we always have a large assortment of Pretenders in store. We have a Shah Shuja all ready to *lâcher* at Dost Mohammed if he does not behave himself, and Runjeet is ready to join us in any enterprise of that sort.' British confidence, however, was not as strong as this suggests. The writer added: 'Still, all these *tendencies* towards war are always rather nervous work. You should employ yourself more assiduously in plucking Russia by the skirts, and not allow him to come poking his face towards our little possessions.'

The comments were made by Miss Emily Eden, sister of the governor-general, Lord Auckland, in a letter to Charles Greville, clerk to the Privy Council, in June 1838. Miss Eden came out to India with her sister Fanny and brother George in 1836; the two maiden ladies and their brother were inseparable. During the six years of Auckland's tenure of office, the trio visited places where European contact was barely twenty years old, and places where no European had ever been before. Both sisters wrote immense numbers of letters home, which were published, causing a minor sensation in England. And no wonder, for they were leading a life virtually unique among women then, and both were well able to describe it. Emily in particular had a perceptive political eye – though she also had an extravagant sense of status. Of Indians, she wrote: 'The poor ignorant creatures are perfectly unconscious what a very superior article an Englishwoman is. They think us contemptible, which is a mistake.'

Now it may sound amusing, but then such attitudes were very real; and it was just such attitudes that led, twenty years later, to one of the worst episodes in the life of British India: the Mutiny. In the meantime, though, Emily travelled with a mixture of homesickness, resigned fortitude and genuine interest that exactly expressed the English approach to India. Undeniably it was a far harder life than the ladies would have had in England; they might be in camp for four and a half months a year – 'the blessing of being in a house again is not to be described' – and in camp, where it seemed to rain every week, 'there was hardly a month free from ague'. Emily wrote with vivid and expressive little images: 'Often our camp would apparently be pitched in a lake . . .'; or with a deep and sometimes absurd nostalgia: '. . . for the past four days we have had unceasing rain, with a great deal of thick white fog, which I greatly affection; somehow it has a smell of London, only without the taste of smoked pea-soup, which is more germane to a London fog, and consequently closer to my patriotic feelings.'

It would be much more difficult now to find a person who could feel patriotic about a thick fog; but the pathos of this 'patriotism' is quite an accurate illustration of the Anglo-Indian frame of mind. There are few places now where a traveller could feel so very far from home and all familiar customs; and the sense of extreme separation and isolation was partly responsible for the over-sensitive reactions to real or imagined threats. Insecurity was one parent of the first Afghan wars, and, a decade later, of the Sikh wars.

The First Afghan War was one of the biggest disasters ever experienced by the British in India. Many books have been written about it; at the time, these attempted to justify and explain it rationally. The justifications and explanations were merely garbled and distorted versions of the truth. Then first-hand accounts began to appear with such titles as *Journal of an Affghan Prisoner;* and then, in reaction to the earlier distortions, historians of the late nineteenth century, acknowledging the immorality and total failure of the war, disclaimed it as 'at once a blunder and a crime'. It was all that, and far more; even the most repentant breast-beating of the 1890s had the unreality of simultaneous under- and over-statement. The unadorned facts were that an unpopular and rejected monarch, unfit to rule, was placed on the throne by force of foreign arms; the current, capable king surrendered and was taken into custody; the replaced king was supported for three years by the arms and money of the foreign power, being quite unable to rule alone; and then, at last, the new régime was utterly defeated by popular rebellion, and by its own incompetence.

Shuja had been installed in Kandahar on 8 May 1839. One of the British sergeant-majors there – William Taylor, of the Fourth Light Dragoons – described the scene.

> In order to give a sort of political éclat to the steps taken to reinstate Shah Soojah on the throne of his ancestors, it was resolved that he

should be solemnly inaugurated at Candahar, and nothing was omitted that could possibly tend to make the ceremony imposing. On the morning fixed for its celebration, the whole of the British forces were paraded in review order on a large plain to the north of the city, whilst the Shah's troops were drawn up at a little distance. In the centre of the field stood a platform canopied with crimson silk, and ornamented with numerous banners and devices, the seat reserved for the Shah being ascended by a broad flight of tapestried steps, and covered with cushions of crimson and gold. The other accessories of the pageant were got up in similar costly style, but the effect, on the whole, conveyed to the mind rather the unsatisfied feeling which attends the hollow show and glitter of the theatre, than the idea of substantial power.

Taylor's estimation of the impotent puppetry was correct. Everyone – the Afghans, the English and Shuja himself – knew that by himself Shuja would not last a week. Everyone knew, that is, except the people who could do anything about it – the English leaders, McNaghten, Burnes and Elphinstone – but they were totally out of touch with the realities around them. McNaghten was blissfully confident that any suspicion of rebellion had vanished in the sunrise of Shuja's second coming; Burnes was convinced that only their presence in Afghanistan was keeping Russia at bay; and Elphinstone, the Commander-in-Chief, was a gentlemanly old invalid, whose illness had so enfeebled his body and brain that he was swayed by each new opinion as easily as a reed in the wind.

Sergeant-Major Taylor's insight did not go very deep, though; he and his dragoons left Kabul very soon after the illusory triumph of Shuja's arrival there. The shah rode into town on 8 August; the Fourth Light Dragoons 'left Cabul on the 14th of September, and arrived at Ghuznee after eight days' march, during which nothing worthy of mention occurred'. Taylor was extremely out of humour at the early departure, because

> Promotion and prize money are the all-engrossing subjects of a soldier's ambition, and this speedy return put an end at once to our long cherished hopes. We well knew that the restless and turbulent spirit of the Affghan chiefs would not permit them to remain long in subjection to Shah Soojah, and that there would consequently be more work for the British troops. Regret and envy of our more fortunate comrades were therefore the predominant feelings which pervaded nearly the whole of the departing troops.

In fact he had no reason at all for envy. Two years and four months later, on 13 January 1842, one exhausted, starving man rode into the British garrison at Jalalabad in India. His name was Dr Brydon, and he was the only survivor of the British force retreating from Kabul. The force had left a week before, 16,500 altogether, troops and camp-followers. A few hundred had been taken prisoner; all the rest had been killed or had frozen, or had starved on the way; and Shuja had been assassinated.

The Durrani unity, the rule of the 'Pearls of Afghanistan', had gone; irrevocably, absolutely and past all pretence. Ranjit, the controlling spirit of the Sikh unity, was dead. There remained only one power in India that could join the subcontinent together.

While British soldiers had been busy propping up Shah Shuja, Emily Eden had been equally busy in her own way – observing, reflecting, commenting and writing. From Calcutta, in February 1841, she wrote to her brother Robert:

> Runjeet's army was a very fine thing, and his kingdom a good kingdom while he was there to keep his one eye upon them, but the instant he died it all fell into confusion, and his soldiers have now murdered all their French and English officers, and are marauding wildly all over the country. It is not actually any business of ours, but it interrupts our communications with Afghanistan; and, in short, it is obvious that it might at last furnish one of those pretences for interference England delights in, and when once we begin I know (don't you?) what becomes of the country we assist – swallowed up whole.

Three o'clock in the morning on a bright moonlit night. The 'General Beat' sounded, and slowly the Bengal Army began to move away from the wreckage of Multan. The line of men, horses, camels, guns, bullocks and carts creaked forward at a steady three miles an hour – 16,000 soldiers, Indians and Europeans; 700 officers; 97 guns. No one counted the number of animals, or the crowds of camp-followers.

The army sang as it marched through the moonlight. The road was hard, but the men were light-hearted, and the song passed cheerfully from one company to the next. Three troops of cavalry; two troops of horse artillery; four companies of foot artillery; three companies of sappers and two of pioneers. The First Brigade – three companies of infantry – remained at Multan; the Second Brigade under Colonel Markham accompanied the rest of the army. There were four companies in that brigade – three of Indian infantry and one of English: the 32nd Foot.

It was an age when war was still thought romantic, when armies in the field glittered with brilliant colours. Even in the pale moonlight they were impressive. The soldiers of the 32nd wore red, white and blue – – white collars and shoulders, white frogging across their chests; a diagonal white cross quartered their bodies. Their shell-jackets – short jackets with a long tail at the back – were bright red, their trousers dark blue with a red line of piping down each leg. They wore tall dark blue hats, peaked, and crested with the number 32. Each man shouldered a musket that stood almost as tall as himself; on each man's back was a knapsack and a small compact bedroll.

The lines of men tramped evenly and regularly along, their songs following the rhythm of their feet. Above their heads the moon was slowly sinking; faint shadows lay behind the creaking gun-carriages, the tall muskets, the ranks of men and animals. Bullocks snorted and wheezed, tugging the supply-carts; camels swayed and sighed with an air of infinite superiority; sometimes a horse whinnied. Row succeeded row, steady and inexorable, and like a gigantic living creature, the army pressed on through the night.

Many of the soldiers were very young, scarcely more than boys. In one company half were aged between twenty and twenty-five. In the 32nd, there was a Private Waterfield, twenty-six years old; he had already soldiered for seven years. He marched as regularly and sang as cheerfully as the rest; he too was elated at their victory at Multan.

When he had joined the army in 1842, Waterfield had been nineteen years old. He had journeyed from Leicester, his home town, as far as Portsmouth, searching for a livelihood. In Portsmouth he had been on the brink of joining the growing navy, until he chanced to meet an old school-friend who was a private in the 32nd. Very swiftly young Robert Waterfield fell in love with the idea of a soldier's life, and after a conversation with a smart young sergeant, Waterfield accepted half a crown in the queen's name, and enlisted.

He had served in Yorkshire first, helping to quell the Chartist riots, and then in Ireland. Soldiering of that sort, as he soon discovered, was tedious and tiring; boredom among the men led to drunkenness, and within his first four months in the army Waterfield had seen so many floggings he wished heartily that he could quit.

It was at the end of May 1846 that his company embarked for India. On the 29th they were taken down through Cork's long, lovely natural

Religious bandits: the Thugs of India (see pages 130 to 133)

Lord Dalhousie

A model of H.M steam ship *Medea* which brought the Koh-i-noor to England

The erection of the Crystal Palace

The exterior of the Crystal Palace, south: 'The blazing arch of lucid glass with the hot sun flaming on its polished ribs and sides shone like the Koh-i-noor itself'

Victoria and Albert at the opening of the Great Exhibition

Chubb's patent diamond case. The diamond is visible in the centre of the glass dome which, at night or in cases of emergency, descended into the base of the cage

The crystal fountain. Many people assumed this was the diamond and were disappointed by the real thing

Victoria and Albert Museum, Bombay

Dhulip Singh by J. A. Goldingham

harbour to the cove where their ship, the *Abouker*, lay; and after a day of becoming used to being on shipboard, they set sail on the morning tide – 4 a.m. on 31 May. It was Whit Sunday.

Most of the troops were instantly struck down by sea-sickness. Waterfield was one of the lucky ones, then and throughout his career in the army, and he found the sea's movement pleasing rather than otherwise. They passed the Bay of Biscay a fortnight after leaving Ireland; after nine weeks, the Cape of Good Hope – and then they were hit by a terrible hurricane, with such a hard and sudden blast that the vessel was nearly upset. The yard-arm nearly touched the water, and they were only saved by the quickwittedness of the first mate, who steered the vessel slightly off her course and took the force of the wind from her. Waterfield was in his hammock at the time, and he stayed there determinedly, wrapped up in blankets; if he was going down, he wanted to go down warm.

But they survived the hurricane and there was little other drama. Once they saw a waterspout, which stayed visible for half an hour; and on other days Waterfield would spend time gazing at the flying-fish, which fascinated him. In all the long weeks of the voyage, no one died, which was a fairly remarkable thing; and one baby – a boy – was born. He was named Abouker, after the ship. On the whole, the voyage was peaceful and calm; and after 112 days' sailing they anchored at Calcutta – on 10 September 1846.

India meant heat and long marches, and, for many of the young soldiers, sudden death. With their feet on dry land once more, they set out on a three-month march to their quarters at Meerut, fifty miles north-west of Delhi. The numerous sick were carried by Indians in shaded litters; on average, the troops covered twelve miles a day. Nothing of great importance to the company occurred throughout the long march; for Private Waterfield, one of the most important things was that he was able to borrow and read a history of the First Afghan War, which he found of great interest.

Stationed as he was between Delhi and the Punjab, Waterfield came to know the immediate history of the area; he knew that chaos and anarchy had followed in the Punjab after Ranjit Singh's death in 1839. He learnt how Kharak Singh – Ranjit's only acknowledged son – had ascended to the throne; how weakly he had ruled; how he was overthrown after only three months by his own son; how the boy was killed within a year, and was succeeded by his own mother, and how she was forced to abdicate by a new pretender. The firecracker series continued until September 1843, when the last of Ranjit's reputed sons was declared sovereign. Dhulip Singh, the son of the dancing-girl and the water-carrier, became Maharajah of the Punjab.

The new maharajah was still a minor; his mother and her latest lover acted as regents. The child probably would have been slaughtered by some other rival quite soon, but, as things turned out, he lived a long and fairly prosperous life as maharajah, and this, paradoxically, was due to a war that removed his authority.

Throughout the anarchical period, the Sikh army, the *khalsa*, had been the one part of the state that had grown steadily more powerful. Simultaneously, British rule of Indian land had expanded, and with some reason the Sikhs began to fear that the Punjab would go under next. It was in an attempt to prevent this that the *khalsa* crossed their southern boundary, the Sutlej. The result was the First Sikh War, from the 18 December 1845 to 10 February 1846, culminating in the battle of Sobraon, in which an estimated 10,000 Sikhs died. It was the climax of the first direct confrontation of Sikh and British; and where 10,000 Sikhs died, 320 British died. The short, sharp war lasted seven weeks; eight days after it was over, Dhulip Singh made a formal submission to the British.

It seemed that the Sikhs' aim of keeping the British at bay had failed completely, for the next logical step was for the British to annex the Punjab into their own dominions. But seven months later, when Waterfield and the 32nd arrived in India, the Punjab was still independent. The reason was simply that the East India Company did not want to rule any more of India. Already it had become something far more than an ordinary joint-stock company; in effect, it was a trading republic, and the directors in London were feeling the weight, and the cost, of their responsibilities. Instead of annexing the defeated state, they wanted to go back to the happy kind of alliance that had existed under Ranjit Singh; and so a British agent was installed at Lahore, and a Sikh council of regency was created to advise the young maharajah until he attained his majority. But not everyone approved of the arrangement – some British were certain that another trial of strength would occur if full dominion was not established; and naturally, there were many Sikhs who deeply resented the British intrusion. Yet it was not a Sikh who made the first resistance; it was a Hindu named Mulraj, the governor of the Punjab's most southerly province, Multan.

The 32nd had arrived outside the walls of the city of Multan on 25 August 1848. They had marched for fifteen days. In their tents at camp the Fahrenheit thermometers read 123°. Twenty-two men had died on the way from heat-stroke and other sicknesses. Sixteen of the twenty-two died in one morning, probably as much from the medical care as from the heat; it was a time when bleeding and blistering were still favourite methods of treating any ailment, and with some dismay Waterfield saw the sick men being bled until they fainted.

Multan was a city well used to siege. With his strong sense of history, Waterfield saw the British siege as the last in an ancient series – following Bin Kasim in the late eighth century, Mahmud of Ghazni in the tenth, Mahomet Ghore in the twelfth, Tamerlane in the fourteenth and Ranjit Singh in 1818. The British siege lasted nearly five months, before Mulraj surrendered; his surrender was unconditional, but when he emerged from the fort, the British troops viewed him with respect – he had done, they said, all a brave man could do, and held out while one spark of chance was left.

Waterfield was glad to leave Multan. During the siege of Multan, very bad fighting had begun in other parts of the Punjab, and while their prisoner was escorted to Lahore, the army moved on. New work awaited them at Gujerat, 235 miles away.

This time the march took twenty-four days; on 20 February the Bengal Army joined Lord Gough's army near Gujerat. Waterfield met an old friend there, a man from Leicestershire, and they had breakfast together – roast beef, mutton, boiled bacon and rum. They talked of their homes in Leicestershire, and of the battle due on the morrow; later that day, they and all the other men were issued with double rations to take on to the battlefield, and then Waterfield spent the evening writing to his parents. He always wrote home before a battle; he felt a little closer then, and it calmed him as well. And with the letter written, the young private went to bed, and slept soundly.

The next morning the entire camp buzzed with action. Soon after dawn everyone was busy striking tents and packing bags. The morning was bright and clear and grew brilliantly sunny, and the army marched confidently to battle. They tramped through fields of standing corn, four feet high and wet with dew, and soon were throughly soaked. After four miles or so, they could see the Sikh army – every hilltop and rise, even the roofs of houses, all were covered with watching men. The British lines were deployed to right and left, and then it began.

For three hours they cannonaded each other, 157 guns roaring as the full artillery of both armies opened up. The British troops were ordered to lie down so that the enemy's shot might pass over them – and behind them, where the hurtling balls hit the ground and bounced, the earth was as torn as a newly ploughed field, and the soldiers were covered with soil. Then, through clouds of smoke, the British advanced, and after the impersonal distant fighting, the personal battles began face to face; the opposing armies suddenly changed from blurred, anonymous ranks to sharply focused groups and individuals, each identifiable, with all the many expressions of people hand-in-hand with death – fear, scorn, desperate courage – all in a mad confusion as bayonets and swords clashed across each other, and men fell together in a deadly embrace, each with his hands tight around the other's throat, and skin and skulls flew in pieces through the air.

In the midst of the chaos some men were able, to their surprise, to observe it all with detachment. A passion something like that of a berserker seemed to take hold of them; they pushed in and ploughed on without fear or restraint – a corporal in the 32nd, John Ryder, said that in such a battle all fear left him, and even though men all around him were falling, he never once thought of dying himself. It was something different from bravery, a passionate detachment, a transcendent rage that made it possible for men to spear and disembowel other men without the slightest horror or hesitation. Some of the Sikhs had the same quality, and after the battle the British remembered them with unfeigned admiration. But the Sikh army, though it outnumbered the British, fought in its habitual defensive manner; the British seemed to concentrate their will into an irresistible offensive. Many of them, in other battles, had seen wounded friends killed by Sikhs, and since the British custom was to spare a wounded man, the memory of those killings inflamed the British so greatly that Gujerat became a battle of revenge. And they all felt the same: at least once the British force all charged in unison without even knowing if an order to charge had been given. And neither side asked for, nor received, any quarter at all.

When it was all over, Waterfield described how parts of the battleground were literally covered with the dead and dying of the enemy. He saw only one dead European – 'at least a part of one', he wrote. 'He was a sergeant of the 2nd Europeans: his cap, grog bottle, and his head was all we saw.' In the 32nd, only one man had been killed; deaths in the whole British army amounted to ninety-six. The whole battle had lasted three and a half hours. For the British force, it was a total victory.

The British had already tried to establish a friendly Indian government in the Punjab; after Gujerat, annexation was almost inevitable. It has often been argued that annexation was deliberately avoided after the First Sikh War in order that the Sikh army might be tempted to rise again, and then be smashed completely, as had happened at Gujerat; but on the whole it seems unlikely that the British thought so far ahead.

Instead, their optimistic and rather simplistic faith in a friendly, Indian-ruled Punjab seems to have been quite genuine; a large part of the army had been disbanded after the first war and activities in general were on a peace-time footing. Even after the second war, annexation was not a foregone conclusion, for the two most important Britons involved – Lord Dalhousie, the young governor-general, and Sir Henry Lawrence, who had been British agent at Lahore between the wars – disagreed profoundly on the best course. Dalhousie favoured immediate and complete annexation; Lawrence, who for three years had been intimately connnected with the Sikhs, believed firmly in the possibility and desirability of a friendly native government. But Dalhousie, though younger and less understanding, was the senior in office; the decision was quickly made and quickly implemented. On 30 March 1849, Dalhousie wrote a letter from Camp Ferozepore, on the south bank of the Sutlej. His representative, the Honourable William Elliot, had arrived at Lahore two days previously on the 28th.

> He saw the Regency and most ably effected his mission; and yesterday, the 29th, the Council of the Regency and the Maharajah signed their submission to the British power, and surrendered the Koh-i-noor to the Queen of England; the British colours were hoisted on the Citadel of Lahore, and the Punjab, every inch of it, was proclaimed to be a portion of the British Empire in India.

Eight

Towards a Greater Unity

Dalhousie and Dhulip Singh – the British claim the Koh-i-noor – controversy in England – John and Henry Lawrence – John Login – the Koh-i-noor is nearly lost – the Thugs – the legend of the passage of the diamond through India – the true story – the diamond leaves India

When the Directors of the East India Company discovered that they had become rulers of an extra 133,000 squares miles of India, they were less gratified than might have been expected. In fact, their reception of the news had a marked air of coolness; they had been delighted by the victory at Gujerat, but to undertake the extra load of rule was not a welcome thought, particularly when it was presented as a *fait accompli*. And it was worse when they realized that Dalhousie's treaty meant they could not keep the Koh-i-noor – 'Blockhead!' they wrote to him. 'Our estimate of each other is mutual,' Dalhousie replied tartly.

The terms of the treaty imposed by Dalhousie on Dhulip Singh were apparently simple. They were these.

> FIRSTLY, His Highness Maharajah Duleep Singh shall resign for himself, his soldiers and his successors, all rights, titles and claims to the sovereignty of the Punjab or to any sovereign power whatsoever.
>
> SECONDLY, All property of the state of whatever description and wheresoever found shall be confiscated to the Honourable East India Company in part payment of the debt due by the State of Lahore to the British Government and of the expenses of the war.
>
> THIRDLY, The gem called Koh-i-noor which was taken from Shah Sooja-ool-Moolk by Maharajah Runjeet Singh shall be surrendered by the Maharajah of Lahore to the Queen of England.
>
> FOURTHLY, His Highness Duleep Singh shall receive from the Honourable East India Company for the support of himself, his relations and the servants of the State, a pension of not less than four

and not exceeding five hundred thousand of the Company's rupees per annum.

FIFTHLY, His Highness Duleep Singh shall be treated with respect and honour. He shall retain the title of Maharajah Duleep Singh Bahadur and he shall continue to receive during his life such portion of the pension above-mentioned as may be allotted to him personally, provided he shall reside at such place as the Govenor-General of India may select.

Simple though the terms appear to be, they found many critics. Not from the Sikhs, nor from people questioning the morality of annexation; those would come later. Dalhousie described thus the two opposing critical views. The Court of Directors of the East India Company were 'ruffled at my having caused the Maharajah to cede to the Queen the Koh-i-noor; while the "Daily News" and my Lord Ellenborough are indignant because I did not confiscate everything to Her Majesty, and censure me for leaving even a Roman pearl to the Court'. He said he felt like a bundle of hay between two asses – an inversion of an old proverb with a pointed reference to his opinion of his critics' intellect. Dalhousie, for his part, was a determined and in a way a simple man. Presented with a problem, he assessed it swiftly according to his own standards, made a decision, and stuck to it. This was a habit that was to earn him many friends and as many critics, with a fair seasoning of enemies; but to be just, it must be said that it was an effective way of going about things, and the effects were not all bad. As far as India was concerned, he joined that group beginning with the Aryans 5,000 years before – the group of people who, one after another, believed that the more of India that came under their sway, the better things would be for all concerned. And by that standard, Dalhousie had prodigious success, and he knew it. After annexing the Punjab, he commented:

> If the Government sanction and approve my act (as unless they are maniacs they must do), their approval must be full and conspicuous. It is not every day that an officer of theirs adds four millions of subjects to the British Empire and places the historical jewel of the Mughul Emperors in the Crown of her Sovereign.

One of his strongest critics at the very beginning was Henry Lawrence, the man who had effectively been sole governor of the Punjab between the wars. Unfortunately for Dalhousie, Lawrence was eminently suited to administer the new province; he was popular with the people, and he cared for them as people. Henry's brother John was a man of comparable ability having been Magistrate of Delhi, and from

Dalhousie's point of view was infinitely preferable; where Henry advocated personal understanding as the basis of rule, John followed a strictly impersonal code. To the one peace and cooperation were the first essentials; to the other, it was a question more of numbers – numbers of subjects, of square miles, of rupees. The brothers could scarcely have been further apart in their understanding of India and their opinions of the Indian people; and Dalhousie made them joint rulers of the Punjab. Together with G. C. Mansel, the brothers made up the Council of Three; and Mansel was unlikely to trouble the governor-general, for he was so consistently able to see *all* points of view in any argument, that – as Dalhousie remarked – he might as well have no point of view at all. Mansel understood his own position rather differently; he seemed to be for ever explaining the ideas of one brother to the other, 'like a buffer between two high-powered steam-engines'.

A fifth Briton came into the picture then, though not as a ruler – John Login, doctor and knight. To him was given the unusual position of being guardian to the young maharajah, whom Login found to be reasonably intelligent, tractable and amiable; and to Login, too, was given charge of the *toshakhana*, the jewel-house of the king. It was there that the Koh-i-noor still rested, after Misr Beli Ram had prevented it going to adorn the brow of Jagannath. The treasurer of Login's day was an old man named Misr Maharaj, and together the two began to put the enormous wealth in order.

> I wish you could walk through that same *toshakhana* and see its *wonders*! The vast quantities of gold and silver, the jewels, both to be valued, so many and so rich! The Koh-i-noor, far beyond what I had imagined; and perhaps above all the immense collection of magnificent Kashmere Shawls, rooms full of them laid out on shelves and heaped up in bales – it is not to be described!

The ecstatic note was written by a cousin of Lady Login's in a letter to her ladyship; she had not accompanied her husband to Lahore. The cousin, who was infinitely impressed, added in astonishment:

> And all this made over to John without *any list*, or public document of any sort, all put in his hands to set in order, value, sell, etc.; that speaks volumes, does it not, for the character he bears, with those whose good opinions are worth having. Few men, I believe, would have been so implicitly trusted.

And Login, it appears, was completely trustworthy. The elderly Misr

Maharaj was considerably relieved by the shift of responsibility, and helped and advised whenever possible. Among other suggestions, he said that if Login showed the Koh-i-noor to any visitor, he should not let it out of his own hand, and he should twist the ribbons that tied it as an armlet around his fingers. Without a doubt, Login's natural honesty was backed up by Dalhousie's policy of material gain for the empire. The governor-general had written to Henry Lawrence, saying that he hoped 'proper precautions' had been taken 'in providing full security for the jewels and Crown property at Lahore'. It would be naïve to pretend that the acquisitive instinct was not as strong in these men as in any other, though they themselves often masked it with virtuous expressions – Dalhousie, for example, regarded his actions as entirely for the benefit of 'her sacred Majesty', Victoria, rather as though the ensuing wealth, fame and honours were unimportant.

From Login the Koh-i-noor went in due course to the Punjab government, the Council of Three, and John Lawrence was entrusted with it. And in all its long history, this was probably the closest the jewel came to being lost for ever, for John was a careless man where jewels were concerned. He found the organization of the enormous new British province far more fascinating than the stone he had been given to look after, and as soon as he had received the diamond he put it in his waistcoast pocket and carried on with his work. He forgot completely and utterly about the gem, and at dinner-time, changing his clothes, he dropped the waistcoat with carefree innocence and went to eat. The rest of the episode has been well told by his biographer, Bosworth Smith, and is worth quoting at length.

> About six weeks afterwards a message came from Lord Dalhousie, saying that the Queen had ordered the jewel to be at once transmitted to her. The subject was mentioned by Sir Henry at the Board, when John said quietly, 'Send for it at once.' 'Why, *you've* got it!' said Sir Henry. In a moment the fact of his carelessness flashed across John's mind. He was horror-stricken, and, as he used to describe his feelings afterwards when telling the story, he said to himself, 'Well, this is the worst trouble I have ever yet got into!' But such was his command over his countenance that he gave no external sign of trepidation: 'Oh yes, of course; I forgot about it,' he said, and went on with the business of the meeting as if nothing had happened. He soon, however, found an opportunity for slipping away to his private room, and with his heart in his mouth, sent for his old bearer and said to him, 'Have you got a small box which was in my waistcoat pocket some time ago?' 'Yes, Sahib,' the man replied, 'I found it and put it in one of

your boxes.' 'Bring it here', said the Sahib. Upon this the old native went to a broken-down tin box, and produced the little one from it. 'Open it', said John Lawrence, 'and see what is inside.' He watched the man anxiously enough as fold after fold of small rags was taken off, and great was his relief when the precious gem appeared. The bearer seemed perfectly unconscious of the treasure which he had had in his keeping. 'There is nothing here Sahib,' he said, 'but a bit of glass!'

Dalhousie wrote to the Queen saying diplomatically that 'the arrangements for the transmission of the Koh-i-noor were incomplete'. John handed the jewel over as fast as possible; and then came the problem of getting it safely to England. There is one marvellously romantic account of this, in which two messengers are sent off simultaneously from Lahore to Bombay, one carrying the jewel and the other acting as a decoy. The one bearing the jewel was, according to the story, disguised as a Moslem merchant; Bombay was 1,300 miles away, and to get there, the messengers had to pass through the heart of the Thug country. The Thugs, like almost everyone else in India, were religious people; unlike many other Indians, however, they had created a religion which actually supported them materially. They were highwaymen of a particularly sophisticated sort – they offered no challenge to stand and deliver, nor did the traveller have the alternative of giving up his money or his life. Instead, murder was to them not only a profession but a fine art. It was an ancient profession; it had flourished in the fifteenth century and probably long before. The Raja of Bargant, through whose territory Tavernier had travelled, had been a Thug of a rather crude and blatant sort; the essence of Thuggee was subtlety, and that raja had been little more than a bandit. In the time of Akbar the Great – the later sixteenth century – many Thugs had been apprehended and executed, but it was not until the 1830s that the British began to suppress them. The officer in charge of the operation was Captain Sleeman – the same man who, as Lieutenant-Colonel Sleeman a decade later, published his *Rambles and Recollections* with its account of the Koh-i-noor.

Sleeman's task was a difficult one – anyone might be a Thug. They did not wear any convenient uniform; there were as many disguises as there were men involved. And the water-carrier could be a Thug; the man who sold textiles in the market might be a Thug; the richest and most respectable citizen of the town could easily be a Thug. Together they would form a band and hunt people like big game, using an elaborate organization. There were four groups within a gang – *Sothaes,* the Enticers, came first. They would select a potential victim – a merchant, a tax-collector, a travelling craftsman, anybody who looked reasonably prosperous – and by one means or another would gain his confidence, and then suggest that (for their mutual protection) they should all travel together. As they travelled they would assess the value of their new companion; they would remain easy-going and friendly, and at last, after a few hours or even several days, the moment would come when the leader of the Thugs would suggest a halt. The moment would not be a casual choice – another group, the *Belhas*, made it their business to select a suitable spot. After all, not every place one passes through can be used as a cemetery.

The caravan would halt then, and all would sit down to eat and rest, to sing and talk and drink. It was not likely that the innocent travellers would notice that each of them had one of the new arrivals at each elbow. A relaxed and friendly period might ensue, with confidences being exchanged; and then a signal would be given, and in a matter of minutes every one of the chosen victims would be dead. They were strangled with a scarf, usually made of yellow silk, and worn or carried by the *Bhuttotes*, the Stranglers, the third group within the gang; and the bodies were stripped and searched by the fourth group, the *Lughaes*.

It did not always happen like that; sometimes the victims would be left completely alone, perhaps without ever knowing that their travelling companions had intended to kill them. For the Thugs were intensely superstitious, and if they happened to meet a maimed man, or a woman with an empty pitcher, at the beginning of a journey, it would all be called off. On the other hand, if an ass happened to bray to the left of the party as they set out, they had every prospect of success. Even then a potential victim might still survive, if he developed a cold on the way, for it was very bad luck indeed to kill a person who was sneezing. Old people were spared, and women, too, but that still left a considerable number of potential victims. The two 'greatest' Thugs that Sleeman encountered each had an average of two murders a month to their debit – one had worked for forty years and killed 931 people; the other had disposed of 508 in twenty years.

For most of the Thugs, loot was only a part of the point of the exercise. The ritual and ceremony involved were at least as important; a simple ambush or casual murder was thought of as wicked and vulgar. And that last word is perhaps the most revealing of the Thug attitude – the main point of an act of Thuggee was that it should be done with style. In that way the whole process became fun. It sounds a gruesome comment, but it is true; and if one forgets moral censure, it is obvious. Thuggee was a hunt and a game. The hunt was made more exciting by the fact that the quarry was intelligent; and the game was made more exciting by being skirted with complex rules. And when the whole was given the religious overlay that is almost second nature in India, it was well-nigh irresistibly attractive.

The disguised British messenger, then, had to carry the Koh-i-noor through hundreds of miles occupied by Thugs; and in him, so it is said, the Thugs saw not only an intelligent quarry, but also one with a prize that had attained a religious value. The story does not tell what became of the decoy messenger, but from the adventures of the bearer, it would appear that the Thugs were not fooled at all; for the bearer had been travelling for only a short while before he was accosted by a man who appeared like himself to be a Moslem merchant. The newcomer wished to travel with the bearer, who refused the offer. It was repeated several times, and at last the bearer of the jewel threatened to shoot his unwelcome companion if he did not leave at once. The companion left, and the British bearer hid in a thicket. Shortly afterwards the other passed by again, this time without his disguise, and the Briton recognized him as a man who had applied for a job as a groom a few days earlier.

Nothing more developed from that incident, but after several days more, the British officer arrived by the side of a river flowing very full and fierce after the rains. It was evening and he could not cross, so he prepared to spend the night on the river bank. Shortly afterwards, two Indians arrived at the same spot, and, seeing the river, asked if they could stay with the officer. They were, they said, members of a certain native regiment on leave.

After eating and talking together, the three lay down to sleep; but the officer was obviously suspicious. Their tale, it seemed to him, did not tally with facts he knew about the regiment to which they said they belonged, and when they lay down to sleep one on either side of him, he decided to be particularly cautious. After they were asleep he moved so that he was no longer in the middle, and lay awake to keep watch. In the early hours of the morning one of the Indians awoke, moved swiftly to the central figure – the second Indian – and strangled him. Then the Briton revealed himself, and, with loaded pistol, forced the living Indian to carry the dead one into the torrent.

Continuing on his way, the bearer of the gem took rest in a roadside inn. A beggar shared the only room with him. Beside each bed was a bowl of drinking-water. There was no apparent reason for wariness, but the bearer placed a thin muslin cloth over his bowl. Awaking in the night, he lit a match and raised the bowl to his lips, taking away the muslin as he did so. On the muslin there was a fine brown powder.

The officer crept over to the bedside of the sleeping beggar, and saw in the light of the matches a long yellow scarf, blood-stained and weighted with a bullet at one end. Leaving his bowl beside the sleeping man, the

Briton slipped out and rode away. Having survived three attempts on his life by the Thugs, he rode on with as little rest as possible, until at last the jewel he carried was safely delivered to Bombay.

It is not at all surprising that this tale should have become part of the accepted mythology of the Koh-i-noor; it seems so appropriate. And it seems so exaggerated that it almost *has* to be true. Even Bosworth Smith, John Lawrence's biographer, hinted at such events when he said that after John handed the jewel over, it 'passed through one or two striking vicissitudes before it was safely lodged in the English Crown'. But, sadly, the tale above is no more than a Victorian gothic-romantic invention, with India as its backcloth – India, which was becoming a symbol to Victorian Britain both of their empire and of all things exotic. The truth of the diamond's journey from Lahore to Bombay was considerably more mundane. A letter written from Simla on 16 May 1850 has this note: 'I could not tell you at the time, for strict secrecy was observed, but I brought it from Lahore myself.' And the writer was Dalhousie.

Had such adventures happened to Dalhousie, he certainly would have let everybody know; and by the same token, had any officer of his made such a journey, the officer would certainly have been honoured. Nevertheless, even the prosaic governor-general left a comment which contains at least the first step of romance.

> I undertook charge of it in a funk [he wrote], and never was so happy in all my life as when I got it into the treasury at Bombay. It was sewn and double-sewn into a belt secured around my waist, one end of the belt fastened to a chain around my neck. It never left me day or night, except once, when I left it with Captain Ramsay (who now has joint charge of it) locked in a treasure-chest, and with strict instructions that he was to sit upon the chest until I came back! My stars! What a relief to get rid of it.

On 6 April 1850, the Koh-i-noor left India. It lay in an iron-bound chest enclosed in a second chest, each chest double-locked, with the keys in the hands of separate people. The treasure was on board Her Majesty's Ship *Medea*, a steam sloop under Commander Lockyer. Formed out of thousands upon thousands of years of silence and darkness, the jewel lay once more in darkness, a mountain of light in an iron chest, surrounded now by the creak of wood and rope and canvas, by the beat of paddles, the hiss of the sea, the shouts of sailors and the night-time quiet of the commander's cabin. Dawns and sunsets rose and faded as they had done for the Aryan invaders of India 5,000 years before, and the ship moved on south and westwards towards the Cape of Good Hope, then north past the African coast and the Bay of Biscay towards Britain.

> How long a time, and they shall be together – Dawns that have shone, and Dawns to shine hereafter?
> She yearns for former Dawns with eager longing, and goes forth gladly, shining with the others.
> Gone are the men who in the days before us looked on the rising of the earlier Morning;
> We, we the living, now behold her brightness, and they come nigh who shall hereafter see her.

With their wisdom, the Aryan poets had touched the heart of things. Dark, light; *Dasyu,* Aryan; night, day and dawn – 'fair-formed, of different hues and yet one-minded, Night and Dawn neither clash nor tarry'. Unity unfolded, flowered and faded with an unending rhythm and balance, the jewel in the heart of the lotus. Through all times and human seasons it moved in silence, through births and lives and deaths of men and women and empires. The Harappans and the Aryans, Porus who had stood against the Greeks, Chandragupta Maurya with the police state and Asoka the benevolent despot; Babur, Akbar, and Aurangzeb the Great Mogul; Nadir the shepherd-king, Ahmad of Afghanistan and Ranjit of the Punjab – all gone. Some had possessed the Koh-i-noor; some, in their conquests, had come close to the role of *chakravartin*, the Universal Emperor. Now, aboard the *Medea*, the jewel moved towards softer landscapes than India, and towards a greater unity; for they were dead who had beheld its brightness, and they came nigh who would thereafter see it.

Nine

O Ful, Tru un Pertikler Okeawnt

The Great Exhibition – Prince Albert – the arrival of the Koh-i-noor in England – it is presented to Queen Victoria and exhibited – popular reactions – the curse on the jewel – Dalhousie's refutation of the curse – the cutting of the jewel – Dhulip Singh sees it again – Victoria is proclaimed Queen-Empress of India

> I wish you *could* have witnessed the 1st *May* 1851, the greatest day in our history, the *most beautiful* and *imposing* and touching spectacle ever seen . . . truly it was astonishing, a fairy scene. Many cried, and all felt touched, and impressed with devotional feelings.

This was from Queen Victoria, writing to her Uncle Leopold, the King of the Belgians.

> The sight from my windows was the gayest and the most gratifying to witness . . . the good humour of all around, the fineness of the day, the manner you were received in both going and coming were quite perfect. We all agreed in rejoicing that the *Foreigners should* have witnessed the affection of the *People* to you and *your family*.

That was from the Duchess of Gloucester, the queen's aunt. And *The Times*, normally so sedate and sensible, became quite carried away with the euphoric tides:

> Never before [said its leading article] was so vast a multitude gathered together within the memory of man. The struggles of great nations in battle, the levies of whole races, never called forth such an army as thronged the streets of London on the 1st of May . . . The blazing arch of lucid glass with the hot sun flaming on its polished ribs and sides shone like the Koh-i-noor itself. Little flags fluttered cheerily along its entire length, their varied colours catching new splendour from the glittering surface, and never did the most fanciful of poets

image a more glorious palace than plain, prosaic England offered to the admiration of the world.

It *was* a glorious palace that England offered – the Crystal Palace, housing the Great Exhibition of the Industry of All Nations. The building itself was one of the largest ever erected; but the statistics of its creation – the acres of land it covered, the tons of metal that supported the acres of glass – are in themselves meaningless. They are numbers so large that they go beyond the understanding of the mind's eye, even in an age when it is common to speak of distances in light-years and to number things in billions. However, if the thought of inter-stellar space boggles the mind and diminishes human importance to nothing, the sight of the Crystal Palace did the opposite. To look at a photograph, or a drawing of it, or to *remember* it before its final blazing destruction, is to have a staggering impression of size, and of a grandeur that does not diminish human importance, but instead glories in all the best things that humanity *can* achieve – the creation and appreciation of beauty, the advance *and control* of technology, the forgetting and renouncing of petty strife and jealousy. For the Great International Exhibition had a double purpose – it was an enormous material show case of technology and industrial achievement, and it was also an immensely courageous attempt to realize an ideal. It was the creation, at the heart of the world's greatest empire, of a place where all the nations of the world could gather harmoniously and display their highest achievement, not in competition, but in admiration. In a way it was easy for the British then to hold such an ideal, for their industrial achievements were two generations ahead of the rest of the world. From their point of view, there was no competition, and hence plenty of room for admiration. Nevertheless, the ideal existed in the conscious thoughts of all those involved. *The Times* commented that the exhibition was 'an occasion which might be celebrated by the whole human race without one pang of regret, envy, or national hate' – and it would be mean and petty to decry it. The irony was that the man who gave birth to the idea of such an exhibition was not British but German – Prince Albert, the husband of Queen Victoria – and he achieved it in the face of general unpopularity and considerable criticism.

The mere fact that Albert had been married to the queen for eleven years, and that they personally were very happy, was not enough to endear him to the British people. His first, and major, handicap was that he was not British. He did not appear to have any of the virtues that the British upper classes prized – he sat badly on a horse (until Victoria taught him); he would organize hunts so that the quarry had no chance of escape; he was a strictly moral person in sexual matters; he drank very little. He had an excellent business brain and he was a superb organizer, but such aspects mattered comparatively little when their owner appeared to the public to be such a cold fish. Both during his life and ever since his death, Albert has been subjected to wildly varying extremes of opinion; the truth lies somewhere in the middle. Victoria as a widow made her dead husband appear to be a paragon of all the classical virtues, a model of goodness, kindness, sense and patience; detractors in his life-time saw instead the cold and unemotional scientific thinker, the cerebral foreigner who preferred instructive reading to light conversation, the depressing efficient man who exercised for health rather than for pleasure. In fact he was all of these and more; the paradoxical characteristics were united in a strong and ultimately overwhelming sense of duty – towards his wife, his family, his native country and his adopted country. Aloof, arrogant, kind, patient, cold, prudish, gentle, loyal, dutiful, distant – he was a thoroughly confusing mixture to anyone who was not in constant close contact with him, which, of course, meant that he confused almost the entire population of Britain. He was foreign, different, incomprehensible, and therefore probably untrustworthy. And so Parliament decided that the queen's husband could not have precedence over dukes, and that his allotted income should not be the £50,000 that Victoria suggested, but only £30,000; and when the prince proposed his vision of the Great Exhibition, Parliment refused to finance the project. It would be a desecration of its proposed setting, Hyde Park; the capital and perhaps the country would be overrun with foreigners; prices in the city would certainly rocket; plague would be imported; riots would ensue when the common people gathered in mass; revolution would be imminent.

However, Albert was determined; and when Parliament failed him, he went ahead with a public subscription, in which the Queen was the first subscriber. It was a slow business, and cartoons appeared showing Albert in the position of a small boy shyly holding out his hat for pennies as grim-faced silhouettes hurried by; but at last the funds were gathered, and in the great park the great building slowly rose.

Portsmouth: June 29th 1850. The *Medea* steam sloop, under Commander Lockyer, arrived at Spithead this morning from China, India and the Cape of Good Hope. She has brought to England Captain Ramsay Military-Secretary to the Governor-General of India, in charge of the Koh-i-noor diamond. The *Medea* has made the fastest passage from the Cape on record, forty days.

The *Medea*'s journey from Bombay to the Cape had not been so easy. On her first day out there had been an outbreak of cholera, and two men had died. Once across the Indian Ocean, Commander Lockyer had put the vessel into Mauritius under quarantine to renew the supples of fuel, food and water; little coal or food was left, and the remaining water was too foul to drink. But though the ship was moored outside the harbour, the Mauritians wanted nothing to do with cholera, and the request for supplies and medicine was refused. The *Medea* remained at anchor overnight and her request was repeated in the morning; this time a lighter was sent out with coal, and 130 tons were taken on board. Neither food nor water were provided, and only a little medicine arrived at the last minute; for, having stayed two days, the *Medea* was ordered to leave or be fired on. 'In this state, ill-found in every essential for the health and comfort of her crew, the *Medea* was driven off to sea.' Heading south-west for the Cape, a heavy gale hit the vessel from the west. Much of the decking was washed away, and 'the main rigging gave out so much that the main mast was very near going over the side'.

After the Cape, the going was smoother. The *Medea* anchored at Spithead exactly twelve weeks after leaving Bombay; and four days later, her precious cargo, the Koh-i-noor, was presented to Queen Victoria by the deputy chairman of the East India Company.

'PRAY GO BACK! All the Roads leading to ye Exhibition are Blocked Up!' That was George Cruikshank's caption to one of his drawings in the summer of 1851. The Exhibition, so hotly opposed and from such an unpopular originator, was a rip-roaring success, unprecedented and almost unbelievable. England's population then was eighteen milllion; before the exhibition closed, after five and a half months, six million people had passed through its gates. Some were foreigners, many were visitors who came again and again, but still that simple statistic indicates the exhibition's intoxicating impact on the country. Special trains were run from the provinces; every day in London, roads were blocked, and all the traffic, pedestrian and horse-drawn, was focused on the Crystal Palace. Everyone was dazzled and delighted.

The Times, in quiet astonishment, said of the first day that

> even people who had never before seen the sun rise, except through a ballroom window, were in full activity soon after dawn, impelled by the impulse that seemed to lend life and energy to the whole substance of the great and somewhat lethargic metropolis . . . If a man ventured

into the Strand or Holborn at eight o'clock with the intent to see the show, he felt half inclined to turn back with the idea that it would be useless to go where 'all the world' would be before him.

It was a magical morning. The crowds had been gathering since first light around the park, though the opening ceremony was not due till noon. Every tree was covered with people striving to see over the milling heads before them. At about a quarter past eleven the sky began to cloud over in a threatening way, and there was a short sharp shower, succeeded by snatches of drizzle, but no one was put off; they were waiting to see the queen, and the 'queen's weather'. Victoria had a knack of appearing just as the sun did, and on that May morning neither she nor Albert nor the people were disappointed. Just before noon, the sun broke out steadily and the rain stopped; and a few minutes later, 'a vision of waving plumes and bright steel came scouring up the Row'. The sun, shining on the moist earth, made the procession into a shimmering misty mirage, a vision of an almost unreal splendour. First came the carriages of the aristocracy, then a troop of Life Guards at a trot; and then the royal carriage – 'and the voices of the people hailed the Queen again and again with hearty cheers, as she came by bowing kindly and graciously'.

Within the Crystal Palace, the scene was even more theatrical, even more exalted and even more touching for all present. On every side were vast complicated machines, statues of all descriptions, carpets and jewels and clothes – everything that could testify to the highest peaks of human skill and craftsmanship and invention. The very building itself was overwhelmingly impressive – fully grown trees spread their branches within it, and yet it still arched higher; and this, it must be remembered, was at a time when St Paul's Cathedral was still the highest point in the London skyline. Thirteen thousand exhibitors from all parts of the world displayed their works in a mile of galleries; and at the centre of it all stood the throne – but no one would have caught the echo of India, or even known how, centuries before and thousands of miles away, Akbar the Great had created his own dream city of Fathepur Sikri, and had placed his throne at its heart.

Already the Crystal Palace was crowded with people: commoners, ladies and gentlemen, in the galleries, dressed in their finest clothes; below them, ranks of armed soldiers in red and black, with gold epaulettes and white plumes; the beefeaters with their archaic uniforms stood close behind the throne, a proud body of men well aware of their past and their intimate connections with the Crown; before the throne, groups of dignitaries of the United Kingdom and of other countries stood in more sober, dark clothes, their top hats in their hands. The heralds, clad in gold with the royal monogram, sounded a fanfare; the royal couple appeared, the queen wearing a dress of pink silk and the prince in the full dress uniform of a field-marshal – and as a last brilliant touch the sun burst out, and a flood of light poured through the glittering arches.

The heralds sounded the notes of the National Anthem; the choir rose and sang; and everyone suddenly burst out cheering. The Great Exhibition of 1851 was on.

The Times next morning made a tactful little comment.

> His Royal Highness Prince Albert [it said] appeared less composed than Her Majesty, and his emotion was visible when the ceremony and its procession had been happily conducted to its close. It was natural that he should feel strongly the termination of a spectacle, the grandest perhaps that the world ever saw, and with which his name and reputation are henceforth inseparably associated.

Many of the six million who were drawn to the wonders of the exhibition came specifically to see the diamond, the fame of which had spread throughout Britain. And many of them felt that if the diamond had been all there was to see, they would have been heartily disappointed. The jewel lay in a gilt iron cage slightly to one side of the centre of the Crystal Palace, and pride of place in the central transept was given to an enormous and strikingly beautiful crystal fountain. Visitors gravitated towards this, and when they turned aside to find the jewel, it seemed tiny by comparison. Among the many guides published to the exhibition, there was one in particular which expressed, in gentle satire, the reaction of many provincial folk to the 'Mountain of Light'.

This guide ran to an edition of 4,000, which was quite surprising, since it was rather difficult to read at first; but it was fun, because it had to be read with a thick country accent, and it was all part of the holiday. Its title was:

O FUL,
<u>TRU un PERTIKLER OKEAWNT</u>
o bwoth wat aw seed un wat aw
yerd, we gooin too the
<u>GREYT EGGSHIBISHUN,</u>
E LUNDUN,
wele kalikilatud fur to giv thoose foke o gradely

> hinseet hinto things, us hassent ad nothur
> toime nur brass fur to goo un see fur
> thersels.

As an account, it was indeed full *and* particular, and it gave a delightful 'hinseet' into the Koh-i-noor. The writer starts off beside the crystal fountain, wondering whether or not that is the famous 'Ko-e-nure'; he is about to ask a bystander, when a woman asks first, and the writer, thanking his lucky stars he has not made a fool of himself, quickly steps in to guide the lady to the jewel.

> Aw seed a greyt glas thing welley th' shap ov o umbrel, un wayter comin eawt uth top on't, un us aw were studdyin obeawt it, thynks aw to mesel, it mun be the greyt Dimun us ov yerd so mich on, un od loike fur to made o foo o mesel we axin o gentelmun iv it wor so, but o wummun just sav't me, we axin im just mete same question afore me. E made onsur un sed, no my gud wummun, this is the Krystil fountun. Whos hoo wer taukin too im aw seed o chap showin onuther felley weere obeawts th' Ko-e-Nure wor, un so aw turnt me reawnd un aw sed, Mistris, the greyt Dimun us theere, under that brass kage. Ther's naut loike o chap avin his wits abeawt im, is ther?

And then, moving along to have a look at the 'greyt Dimun', the writer of this erudite guide had a disappointing surprise.

> O poleesmun wor takkin kare uth Dimun, un it wor in a kage loike a pol-parrot. Aw dar sa us yo'l thynk us om umbuggin yo, wen aw sa us this greyt Dimun koed Ko-e-Nure, us ther's bin sich o greyt din abeawt, is no biggur, nur ardly as big, us o bo o coblur's wax ur o kidney pottato, un, fur o that, they sen us its wurth too milliuns o peawnds. Waw, fur any mak o use us it ud be to me, aw wodent potter eawt foive shillin for't.

Others were disappointed too, though for different reasons. The *Illustrated London News* published several accounts of the exhibition, including a magnificent poster given free with the magazine, and while they acknowledged the beauty of the various jewels included in the show, and thanked their owners for exhibiting them, they regarded the Koh-i-noor as 'gigantic, but somewhat rough and unhewn'. Previously when Europeans had seen the Koh-i-noor it had been an Indian possession; the Indian aesthetic had remained unchallenged since

Aurangzeb had retrieved the stone from Borgio. But its new owners saw beauty differently.

> A diamond [the *Illustrated London News* explained] is generally colourless, and the finest are quite free from any speck or flaw of any kind, resembling a drop of the purest water. The Koh-i-noor is not cut in the best form for exhibiting its purity and lustre, and will therefore disappoint many, if not all, of those who so anxiously press forward to see it.

Many people, including Prince Albert, agreed with this opinion. The magazine continued:

> The shape of the Koh-i-noor is that of a pear, or rather more oblong; and it would be much reduced in size if cut by a European diamond merchant. Its marketable value would however be increased. It would probably become, if properly treated, one of the finest diamonds now in Europe.

Along with these comments, the magazine published pictures of the jewel in what was termed its 'original setting' – that is, the armlet, flanked with two lesser gems, in which Ranjit Singh had mounted it – and also in its arrangement for the exhibition. Back in India, Dalhousie followed proceedings with great interest, and wrote to a friend in England, saying, 'I see all sorts of sketches and pictures announced of the contents of the Exhibition. If you can get me anything representing *well* the Koh-i-noor in its cage, coloured, I shall be much obliged.'

Apart from the direct bearing the jewel had had on his life in India, there was a further reason for his continuing interest. The year before, shortly after the diamond had been presented to the queen, a retired lieutenant of the 10th Hussars, a man named Pate, lost his reason and had attacked the queen, striking her over the head with a stick. Already some people had heard vaguely of superstitions attached to the stone, and one at least decided that it was all Dalhousie's fault. The governor-general was very indignant, and replied:

> Apparently the several sad and foul events in England lie at my door, as I have sent the Koh-i-noor which always brings misfortune to its possessor. Whoever was the exquisite person from whom you heard this (nobody could be so stupid except Joseph Hume), he was rather lame on both his history and tradition. Without going back to the first emperors who held it, I would observe that Nadir Shah who

took it was usually reckoned well-to-do in the world throughout his life, and that Ranjit Singh has usually been thought to have prospered tolerably. As for tradition, when Shah Soojah, *from whom it was taken,* was afterwards asked, by Ranjit's desire, 'what was the value of the Koh-i-noor?' he replied, 'Its value is *Good Fortune,* for whoever possesses it has been superior to all his enemies.' Perhaps your friend would favour you with his authority, after this, for his opposite statement.

No opposite authority was forthcoming, although anyone could have interpreted historical fact to suit the superstition of his fancy. Gradually it became an accepted standard that bad luck would befall a man who wore the jewel, while good luck would follow a woman. But Dalhousie had been very upset that anyone should attribute the queen's misfortune to him, and in the last letter he wrote to her from India, dated 15 May 1850, he told her the story of Shah Shuja, and ended by saying, 'The Governor-General very respectfully and earnestly trusts that Your Majesty in your possession of the Koh-i-noor may ever to continue to realize its value as estimated by Shah Soojah.'

Shuja's estimation, that the stone was a symbol of good fortune, was as good as any other, and better than many, for the value placed on any gemstone of that size is arbitrary. The severe practicality of living could make it seem valueless to a peasant – 'aw wodent potter eawt foive shillin for't', the anonymous writer of the *Pertikler Okeawnt* had written. And diamonds *are* singularly indigestible. At the other extreme, Agha Mohammed had blinded 20,000 people in his search for the stone. The business-like comment of the *Illustrated London News,* that 'its marketable value would be increased' if it were cut by a European artist, was only true to a limited extent, for even if someone were found who was rich enough to buy such a jewel, its owner still had to be willing to sell it; and, as Babur's son Humayun had said centuries before, 'Such jewels cannot be bought. Either they are won in battle, or they are passed on as an honourable gift.' Above all was the simple fact that this was the Koh-i-noor. There were already diamonds comparable to it in size and purity in Prince Albert's day, and now there are a good many bigger and of even higher quality; but it was not just a big diamond, it was *the* diamond, the 'Greyt Dimun', and it had its own immeasurable and intangible worth as a symbol of *values* more abstract than money and more lasting than hunger.

And yet, at the same time, it was a jewel to be handled and worn and admired. If it seemed rough and unhewn to its new owners, the obvious answer was to cut it to a more appealing shape; and in 1852, after the exhibition had been dismantled, the Koh-i-noor was entrusted to Garrard's of London. Naturally Prince Albert took a close interest in the process.

It was decided that there was not a craftsman in England able to undertake the cutting of the jewel, and a Dutch cutter, Voorsanger, was brought over from Amsterdam. It was a nerve-tearing operation; everyone was aware that, as the *Illustrated London News* had said, the diamond had to be 'properly treated'. The jewel weighed 186.06 carats then; Voorsanger worked for thirty-eight days, and when he had finished, eighty carats had been removed, at a cost of £8,000.

Ornamental diamonds are usually cut in one of two ways, either 'rose' or 'brilliant'. A rose-cut diamond is thinner and flatter than a brilliant-cut; the brilliant has a smaller surface area but is deeper, and because of this the play of light upon the jewel is fuller and finer, and the diamond sparkles more than a rose-cut gem. The choice of cut is generally determined by the natural form of the jewel in question; the Koh-i-noor, in Voorsanger's hands, was cut as a rose. It had been reduced to a weight of $106\frac{1}{16}$ carats – it was still a large diamond, but to Mir Jumla or Shah Jehan, it would have seemed pretty small. When one remembers their diamond, the 'Great Mogul', the monster diamond of $787\frac{1}{2}$ carats, and how it had been ground by Borgio to half its original size when it should have been kept as large as possible, one can realize how unpopular the Venetian's work was. And though the Dutchman, Voorsanger, was working to a different aesthetic, his results were scarcely more popular. Many people felt that a great opportunity had been missed; Dalhousie, for example, wrote regretfully, 'It is badly *cut*: it is rose- and not brilliant-cut, and of course won't sparkle like the latter.' Others thought the whole notion of cutting it was a mistake, and called it 'a most ill-advised proceeding'. But cut it was, and there was no going back; and if, as an ornamental gem, its greatest potential beauty had been missed, it still remained the Mountain of Light.

To an Indian it would have been almost unrecognizable, with its new facets and angles. One Indian in particular, who had known it well, saw it – Dhulip Singh, the disinherited infant maharajah of the Punjab, now grown to manhood and living in Britain under the care of Sir John and Lady Login. The young man was one of the darlings of English society; he was rich, very handsome, very exotic, and yet by this time very English. He was acquiring property in England, he was being tutored in the art of living as an English country gentleman, and he had adopted Christianity. His portrait was being painted, and for the sittings he would go to Buckingham Palace. Whenever he was there the subject of the Koh-i-noor was tactfully avoided, since everyone was aware that to him especially it was far more than an ornament. He knew that it had been recut, and had appeared very interested in the idea, but he had not seen the result – nor, indeed, had he seen the jewel since it left Lahore, chained and belted to Dalhousie's waist. Victoria wondered if he would *like* to see it again, and asked Lady Login to find out, as diplomatically as possible. Her ladyship did so, and Dhulip Singh's reported reply was that he would give a great deal to hold it again in his own hands. Lady Login asked why; and his reason, so she told the queen, was this. The maharajah had replied, 'I should like to take it in my power, myself to place it in her hand, now that I am a man. I was only a child then when I surrendered it to Her Majesty by the Treaty, and now I am old enough to understand.'

What it was that the maharajah now understood was not made clear, but on his next visit to the palace, as he posed on a dais for the portrait, Victoria came up to him and slipped the jewel into his hands. It was quite unexpected and the young man was taken aback. The painting stopped, and he moved to a window and held the diamond in the light, gazing at it eagerly. He inspected it for a quarter of an hour, commenting on its smaller size and increased brilliancy; the others in the room watched him anxiously. At last he turned again towards the queen, bowed low and gave it back to her; and as he did so he said that it gave him immense pleasure to be able to place the great diamond personally in his sovereign's hands.

Prince Albert died ten years after the opening of the Great Exhibition, worn out by overwork following what he saw as his 'duty'. After his death, Victoria, who had adored him, began creating the legend of Albert the Good; and though everyone – or most – acknowledged the justness of his title, the queen's mourning for her husband went on much too long in the popular opinion. But it had been a devastating blow for her – she had almost literally worshipped Albert, and had always had one person to support her in the very hard work of being queen. Before her marriage, Lord Melbourne, the prime minister, had been a close friend and adviser. Victoria's father, the Duke of Kent, had died when she was only eight months old, and Melbourne – '*dear* Lord Melbourne' – filled the emotional gap admirably. After Albert's death there was no one similar. For a while Victoria found some emotional support in the close friendship of John Brown, who had been ghillie to the royal couple in their holidays in Scotland; he was an unpopular man, and their friendship was regarded as scandalous – gossip gave the queen a new name, Mrs Brown – and Victoria still had no statesman for whom she felt a high regard. But then Disraeli became prime minister, for the second time; and, in him, the Queen found a good friend and a good administrator. And it was through his efforts that she became, in title as well as practice, an empress.

By this time British rule extended over a quarter of the world. In India, Victoria had been sovereign of ever-growing areas with the East India Company as their direct ruler, but after the mutiny of 1857, the British government had assumed direct control, and on 1 May 1876 – twenty-five years to the day after the opening of the Great Exhibition – Victoria was named *Indiae Imperatrix*: Empress of India.

The formal announcement of the news was made in India seven months later, on 1 January 1877, at a Grand Durbar in Delhi. All the possible splendour and pageantry of England and India was brought into play, and the viceroy, Lord Lytton, read the queen's address to the assembly.

> We, Victoria, by the grace of God Queen of the United Kingdom, Queen-Empress of India, send through our viceroy, to all our officers, civil and military, and to all princes, chiefs and peoples now at Delhi assembled, our Royal and Imperial greeting, and assure them of the deep interest and earnest affection with which we regard the people of our Indian Empire. We trust that the present occasion may tend to unite in bonds of yet closer affection ourselves and our people; that from the highest to the humblest all may feel that under our rule the principles of liberty, equity and justice are secured to them; and that to promote their happiness, to add to their prosperity and to advance their welfare, are the ever-present aims and object of our Empire.

They were high aims, meant seriously and sincerely; the degree to which they were achieved is a matter of debate that goes beyond the scope of this book. Victoria had a strong sympathy for and understanding of her Indian people, and one of the reasons for her assumption of the imperial title was that she felt it would mean more to them if she were their empress, and not merely the monarch of a distant land. In this intuitive guess, she was very probably correct; not only was India drawn directly into her title, so that she was now specifically ruler of India as well as of the United Kingdom, but also that title was an imperial one. With her, the ancient Indian ideal of the *chakravartin*, the Universal Emperor, came as close as it ever had to complete fulfilment.

Ten

A Certain Tragedy

The problem of ownership of the Koh-i-noor

It would be pleasant to leave the story of the Koh-i-noor at that point – with the diamond, the symbol of unity and eternity, gracing a woman whose rule spanned the world, and whose empire seemed likely to last indefinitely. It would be pleasant, but it would not be realistic. The queen-empress died, and forty-five years after her death the empire ended; and, almost immediately, a question was raised that had never entered the story before: namely, whose true property was the Koh-i-noor?

The question had never occurred before because there had never been any doubt before. In Humayun's words, 'Such jewels cannot be bought. Either they are won in battle, or they are passed on as an honourable gift.' And always, from the first, ownership had been unequivocal. Whenever a switch was made, the previous owner was left in no doubt that he had lost the jewel, and no suggestion was entertained that a new owner should return it. In Britain, the jewel passed from Victoria to Edward VII, George V, the uncrowned Edward VIII and then to George VI. In 1937, when he married, the Mountain of Light was set in the crown of his queen, Elizabeth. It remains there today, and is worn on state occasions by Her Majesty the Queen Mother.

A decade after the jewel was mounted in the State Crown, India became independent of Britain. The country was in a position unique in its entire history: for the first time, it was a united self-governing republic, free in theory of any internal or external monarchical rule. It was a position of great promise, a position whose full implications are still being worked out.

The British Empire, too – and especially the British Empire in India – was unique; apart from its size, its peculiar dignity was that it was the only one of the world's empires to end comparatively peacefully. Transfers of power were usually effected with the flags still flying.

The reason for this lay partly in the way the empire had grown. It had been largely an accidental creation; certainly at various points various individuals had set out with the express intention of adding land and people to the list, but, by and large, ever since the early days of the East India Company and before, administrative additions had been the necessary and frequently unwelcome consequences of commercial predominance. Much of the empire was regarded as an embarrassment rather than an asset by its administrators in London; but once administration was undertaken, it was usually with the aims that Victoria expressed – the happiness, prosperity and welfare of the people.

In short, although many people and incidents could be cited to contradict this, the men and women who ran the British Empire did so – or at least *tried* to do so – according to the morals of the day. And that was where the difficulty lay concerning the Koh-i-noor, for few people were sure whether it had been 'won in battle, or passed on as an honourable gift' – or both, or neither. The problem had been created by Dalhousie.

The battle of Gujerat had been a swift, decisive and complete victory for the British Army over the *khalsa*. The annexation that followed was almost equally swift and decisive. The core of the question, in an empire that ostensibly prized legality and morality above all, was whether it had been either legal or moral; many felt it was neither. The issue was raised in the 1880s, at a time when British sovereignty over India could scarcely have seemed more secure. Arguments were put forward on both sides, and it is a curious fact that the most vocal opponent of the annexation was British, while its most vocal defenders were Indian.

In 1882, a certain Major Evans Bell published a small, but eloquent and persuasive book, called *The Annexation of the Punjab and the Maharajah Duleep Singh*. His basic argument was that the 'conquest' of the Punjab after Britain's early liberal attitude (the peace following the First Sikh War) was a myth, and that the reality sprang from a mixture of Dalhousie's wish for self-aggrandisement and British economic needs. In other words, he argued that the British role between the two Sikh wars was that of *agent provocateur*, and that the regrouping of the *khalsa* was indeed allowed in order that it might be smashed completely. To support his argument, he reminded his readers that in 1848 the British government was the guardian of Dhulip Singh, and that in the rebellion of the *khalsa* this charge 'was never interrupted or disturbed for a single hair by any incident of the rebellion, or by any military operation in or near the capital city of Lahore'. Consequently, in 1849, Dhulip Singh was not 'an object of bounty but one who was in full and legal possession of a sovereignty, with whom "terms" equivalent to a Treaty of territorial cession were concluded, which gave something like regularity and legality to what would otherwise have borne an aspect of naked lawlessness, and to what was in fact no "conquest", but a violent breach of trust'.

Dalhousie's opinion was that the war had involved not merely the *khalsa* but the state of Lahore; in 1848 it had been recorded that he 'considers the State of Lahore to be, to all intents and purposes, directly at war with the British Government'. This was followed by a proclamation saying that all those innocent of participation in the rebellion would be unharmed in any way. It had been proved that instigation of the rebellion led directly to the palace, where the young maharajah's mother was closely implicated; but Dhulip Singh himself was a minor, and hence regarded as legally innocent of complicity. The Koh-i-noor was regarded as a possession of the state, and hence its appropriation was a consequence of the 'direct war' between the *khalsa* and the British government. And there the matter might have rested, as a simple war of conquest and the appropriation of state property; but some of the Britons involved, including Lady Login, were worried. They felt that perhaps the diamond had not been state property, but Dhulip Singh's personal possession, and from this grew the tale of his presentation of the jewel to Victoria. The *facts* of the story are true; it is their *interpretation* that is open to criticism. Dalhousie, in typical forthright style, was openly critical, and in 1854 he wrote:

> Login's talk about the Koh-i-noor being a present from Dhulip Singh to the Queen is arrant humbug. He knew as well as I did that it was nothing of the sort, and if I had been within a thousand miles of him he would not have dared to utter such a piece of trickery.

Dhulip Singh joined in the bickering. He began to refer to Victoria as 'Mrs Fagin', saying she had as much right to the Koh-i-noor as he had to Windsor Castle. But he made no public statement until 1882, by which time he had bought the estate of Elveden in Essex. The cost of living in England was proving high, and in a plaintive series of letters to *The Times* he put forward his pleas, denied by Parliament, for a higher allowance and restitution of the property he had owned as full maharajah. Nothing came of these pleas; *The Times,* commenting in its leading article, said:

> An argument which starts from the sovereign claims of the son of the Lion of the Punjab ends, somewhat ridiculously, though not without a touch of pathos, with the sorrows of the Squire of Elveden . . . There really is a certain tragedy about the whole affair.

In 1953, just before the coronation of Queen Elizabeth II, the question of ownership was brought up once more by India. Many Indians saw the Koh-i-noor as the embodiment of the spirit of their country. When the subcontinent was ruled by Victoria, it had seemed natural that she should hold the symbol of sovereignty; now, it was argued, that Britain had no sovereign rights over India, should not the Koh-i-noor be returned? All of a sudden it became very clear that the diamond had attained an emotional value for the British that they had never previously suspected. There was a prolonged outburst in the national press, in which a rough analysis of the legal and historical tale was made. By then Pakistan, which incorporated Lahore, had emerged as a separate state, and the journalists posed several obvious and pertinent questions. If the jewel should be returned to anyone, why not to the new state of Pakistan, since Lahore was in its territory? This bluff was called in 1977, when Pakistan *did* ask for the jewel. But Dhulip Singh had been head of the Sikh commonwealth; perhaps the Sikhs had a claim. And what of Afghanistan's possible claim? Or Iran's? The field was rapidly expanded. Should the Elgin marbles be returned to Greece? Should any of the other innumerable treasures in Britain be returned to the nations of their origin? Should, indeed, the treasures of the world in general be returned to their sources?

All the arguments served both to fog and to clarify the issue, for, as people became aware of the wider implications, the Koh-i-noor itself tended to be forgotten. One line of thought in Britain was that if India wanted the jewel, its return should have been requested in 1947, when independence was granted. In 1953, both countries were still too close to the imperial days for any unemotional discussion to be held; the empire was still a personal experience for millions of people, both British and Indian. On such a sensitive topic, people tended to see things in very distinct terms – the British Empire, even the concept of empire, was either all good or all bad – and it must be remembered that not all the supporters of empire were British, nor were all its opponents Indian. But to see such a widespread and varied phenomenon as the British Empire – even, indeed, to see the *theory* of empire – as either *wholly* good or *wholly* bad, is absurd.

The awareness of the moral dilemma was not a product of the twentieth century. In 1873, the Crown Princess Victoria had written to her mother, Queen Victoria, saying:

> The right of conquest is a very hard one. God knows I am *not* one who admires it, but *it has* often been, Often, of the Greatest use. England's empire over the East has been the best example of it, and

even *there* Englishmen have NOT always shown themselves as scrupulous, humane, civilized and enlightened as they *should* have done.

Even earlier, in 1840, Vigne had written in his *Visit to Afghanistan*:

> Few can be quite insensible to the glories of a victory, but all admit that triumph is dashed with misery; and battle, victory and triumph are common, and no novelties.

To Dalhousie, the Koh-i-noor was 'the symbol of victory and empire'; to the peoples of the Indian subcontinent, it represented the heart of their country. That is why the wrangling still goes on: people are not arguing over a jewel, a piece of compressed carbon, something that can be bought and sold; they are arguing for possession of a symbol. But the arguments involved are backward-looking and destructive, the wilful opening of old wounds against national pride and honour. This is the saddest part of the whole story, for the eternal diamond could easily be the emblem for a unity far greater than any imperial rule. The classical definitions of tragedy and comedy are that tragedy ends in division and separation, while comedy ends in union and reconciliation. It is nearly 100 years since *The Times* made its regretful comment on the 'tragedy' of the Koh-i-noor. The jewel itself is not likely to leave Britain, since British law forbids that the State Crown should go beyond British shores, and it is highly improbable that the crown will be dismantled; but, if Britain and India could finally accept both the good and the bad in their joint histories, then the tragedy may yet be turned into comedy.

Select Bibliography

Auboyer, Jeannine, *The Art of Afghanistan*, Trans. P. Kneebone, Hamlyn, Feltham, 1968

Baird, J. G. A. (Ed.), *Private Letters of the Marquess of Dalhousie*, William Blackwood and Sons, Edinburgh and London, 1910
Basham, Thomas Llewellyn, *The Wonder that was India*, Sidgwick and Jackson, London, 1967, 3rd edition (first published 1954)
Bell, Thomas Evans, *The Annexation of the Punjab and the Maharajah Duleep Singh*, Trübner and Co., London, 1882
Benjamin, Samuel Green Wheeler, *Persia*, T. Fisher Unwin, London, 1888
Benson, A. C., M.A. and Viscount Esher (Eds), *Letters of Queen Victoria*, vol. II, John Murray, London, 1908
Betjeman, Sir John, *Victorian and Edwardian London from Old Photographs*, Batsford, London, 1969
Bosworth, Clifford Edmund, *The Ghaznavids: Their Empire in Afghanistan and Eastern Iran 994–1040*, Edinburgh University Publications, 1963

Chaudhuri, Nirad Chaudra, *The Continent of Circe: being an essay on the Peoples of India*, Chatto and Windus, London, 1965
Collins, William Wilkie, *The Moonstone*, first published by Tinsley Brothers, London, 1868
Cook, Colonel H. C. B., *The Sikh Wars: The British Army in the Punjab 1845–9*, Leo Cooper, London, 1975

Dickinson, Violet, *Miss Eden's Letters edited by her great-niece Violet Dickinson*, Macmillan and Co., London, 1919
Dowson, J. (Ed.), *The History of India as told by its own Historians*, edited from the posthumous papers of Sir H. M. Elliot. First published London, 1867-7
Duff, David Skene, *Albert and Victoria*, Muller, London, 1972
Dunbar, Janet, *Golden Interlude: The Edens in India 1836—42*, John Murray, London, 1955
Durand, Sir Henry Mortimer, *Nadir Shah, A Romance*, Archibald Constable and Co., London, 1908

Edwardes, Michael Francis Harper, *Everyday Life in Early India*, Batsford, London, 1969
   Indian Temples and Palaces, Hamlyn, London, 1969
   A History of India, Thames and Hudson, London, 1961
   The Necessary Hell: John and Henry Lawrence and the Indian Empire, Cassell, London, 1958

Ettinghausen, Richard, *Turkish Miniatures*, Collins, London, 1965
Eyre, Sir Vincent, *Journal of an Affgan Prisoner*, Routledge and Kegan Paul, London, 1976 (first published 1843)

Farrington, Oliver Cummings, *Famous Diamonds*, Chicago Field Museum of Natural History, 1929
Fraser of Inverness, James, *The History of Nadir Shah, formerly called Thamas Kuli Khan . . . Emperor of Persia*, London, 1742

Gardner, Robert Brian, *The East India Company, a History*, Hart-Davis, London, 1971
Gibbs-Smith, Charles Harvard, *The Great Exhibition of 1851*, HMSO (Victoria and Albert Museum), London, 1950
Giles, A. A. (trans.), *The Travels of Fa-hsien 399–414 or Record of the Buddhistic Kingdoms*, Cambridge University Press, 1923
Godden, John and Rumer, *Shiva's Pigeons: an Experience of India*, Photographs by Stella Shead, London, Chatto and Windus, 1972
Griffin, Sir Lopel Henry, 'Ranjit Singh' from *Rulers of India* by Sir W. W. Hunter, Clarendon Press, Oxford, 1890 etc.
Griffiths, John Charles, *Afghanistan*, Pall Mall Press, London, 1967

Habib, Muhammad, *Sultan Mahmud of Ghazni*, Bombay, 1927
Habibullah, Abul Barkat Muhammad, *The Foundation of Muslim Rule in India: the Establishment and Progress of the Turkish Sultanate of Delhi 1206–1290*, (2nd edition), Allahabad, 1961
Hambly, Gavin Richard Grenville, *Cities of Mughal India: Delhi, Agra and Fathehpur Sikri*, Elek Books, London, 1968
Humphreys, Travers Christmas, *Buddhism*, Penguin Books, Harmondsworth, 1951

Lane-Poole, Stanley, 'Babur' and 'Aurangzeb' from *Rulers of India* by Sir W. W. Hunter, Clarendon Press, Oxford, 1890 etc.
Lannoy, Richard, *The Speaking Tree: A study of Indian Culture and Society*, Oxford University Press, London, 1971
Latif, Muhammad, *History of the Punjab*, Calcutta, 1891
Lee-Warner, Sir William, *The Marquis of Dalhousie*, vol. I, Macmillan and Co., London, 1904

Markham, Sir Clements Robert, *A General Sketch of the History of Persia*, Longmans, London, 1874
Martin, Arthur Palchitt, *Isle of Wight: a personal memoir of Her Majesty at Osborne*, Henry Sotheran and Co., London, 1898
McCrindle, John Watson, *Ancient India as described by Megasthenes and Arrian*, Calcutta, 1877
Mookerji, Radha Kumud, *Fundamental Unity of India*, Bombay, 1954

Narasimhan, Chakravarthi Uijiaraghavn, *The Mahabharata*, Columbia University Press, 1965
Nazim, Muhammed, *The Life and Times of Sultan Mahmud of Ghanzni*, Cambridge University Press, London, 1931

Osborne, Lord William Godolphin, *The Court and Camp of Runjeet Singh*, Oxford University Press, 1973

Prawdin, Michael, *The Builders of the Mughal Empire*, George Allen and Unwin, London, 1963

Robinson, Sir Frederick Percival, K.C.B., *The Trade of the East India Company from 1709–1813*, Cambridge University Press, 1912

Sale, Lady Florentia, *The First Afgan War* [*A Journal of the disasters in Affganistan 1841–2*], edited by Patrick Macrory, Longmans, London and Harlow, 1969
Sen, K. M., *Hinduism*, Penguin, Harmondsworth, 1961
Sen, N. B., *History of the Koh-I-Noor*, New Book Society of India, New Delhi, 1953
Sen, S. P., *The French in India 1763–1816*, Calcutta, 1958
Sitwell, Dame Edith, *Victoria of England*, Faber and Faber, 1937
Sleemman, Sir William Henry, K.C.B., *Rambles and Recollections*, vol. I, Hatchards, London, 1844
    Journey through the Kingdom of Oudh in 1849, London, 1858
Spear, Thomas George Percival, *The Nabobs: A Study of the Social Life of the English in eighteenth century India*, first published Oxford University Press, London, 1932
Spear, Thomas George Percival and Romila Thaper, *A History of India*, Penguin, Harmondsworth, 1965–6
Streeter, Edwin William, *Precious Stones and Gems, their history and distinguishing characteristics*, first published London, 1877
    The Great Diamonds of the World, their History and Romance, G. Bell and Sons, London, 1882
Swinson, Arthur and Donald Scott, (Eds), *Memoirs of Private Waterfield, Soldier in Her Majesty's 32nd Regiment of Foot, Duke of Cornwallis's Light Infantry 1842–57*, Cassell, London, 1968
Sykes, Sir Percy Molesworth, *A History of Persia*, Macmillan and Co., London, 1915

Tagore, Rabindradoth (trans.), *One Hundred Poems of Kabir*, Macmillan, India, Madras, 1973
Tavernier, Jean-Baptiste, *Les Six Voyages* (3 vols.), first published in England by Dr Daniel Cox, London, 1677–8
    Travels in India, translated from French edition of 1676 with a biographical sketch by V. Ball, Macmillan and Co., London, 1889. Second edition edited by William Crooke, Oxford University Press, 1925
Taylor, Colonel Philip Meadows, *Confessions of a Thug*, first published by Richard Bailly, London, 1839, World Classics, 1917
Trevelyan, George Macauley, *English Social History*, Longmans, London, 1944

Vigne, Godfrey Thomas, *A Personal Narrative of a visit to Ghuzni, Kabul and Afghanistan, and of a residence at the Court of Dost Mohamed*, Whittaker and Co., London, 1840

Watters, Thomas, *On Yuan Chwang's (Hsuan Tsang's) Travels in India 629–645*, edited by T. W. Rhys Davids and S. W. Buschen, Royal Asiatic Society, London, 1904–5
Watts, Alan Wilson, *The Way of Zen*, Thames and Hudson, London, 1957
Woodruff, Philip, *The Men Who Ruled India—The Founders*, Jonathan Cape, London, 1953
Wu, Nelson Ikon, *Chinese and Indian Architecture: the City of Man, the Mountain of God, and the Realm of the Immortals*, Prentice Hall International, London, 1963

    Other texts consulted include:
    The Cambridge History of India, vols. 4 and 5
    The History and Culture of the Indian Peoples vol. 6
    The Royal Asiatic Society Journal 1921
    The Times
    The Illustrated London News

Index

AFGHANS, THE, 77, 79, 81–4, 89, 94, 97, 106, 109, 114, 117–18
Afghanistan, 78, 90–8, 103, 107–9, 114, 116, 119, 150
Agha Mohammed Khan, 91–2, 102, 143
Ahmad Shah Abdali (also Durrani), 90–1, 93–5, 98, 101, 104, 134
Akbar the Great, 45–50, 71–2, 76, 130, 134, 139
Akrura, 20–2
Albert, Prince Consort, 136–7, 139–40, 142–5
Alexander the Great, 25–8, 82
Ali Quli Khan (Adil Shah), 89–91
Amritsar, 107, 110, 115
Asoka, 32–3, 37, 46–7, 134
Asvatthama, 26
Aurangzeb, 51, 53; and Tavernier, 54, 60–1; shows diamond to Tavernier, 62–6; 73, 75; his religious convictions, 76–7; his death, 77–8; 84, 100–1, 104, 134, 141
Auckland, 110–11, 116

BABUR, founder of Mogul Empire, his descent, character and life, 38–48; wins a large diamond, 43; 50, 52, 73, 82; compared with Ahmad Shah Durrani, 94–5; 106, 134
'Babur's diamond', 43, 45, 53, 62–4
Balarama, 19–22
Ball, Dr Valentine, 63, 64
Bargant, Raja of, 58, 130
Bell, Major Evans, 148–9
Bernier, François, 51, 60
Bombay, 74–5, 130, 133, 138
Borgio (cutter of 'Great Mogul'), 62, 141
Brahma, 24
Brahmans, 15, 19, 23–4, 31
Buddha, 30, 31, 33

Buddhism, 25, 30, 31, 32

CALCUTTA, 75, 119, 121
Caste, 23, 24
Catherine of Braganza, 74
Chakravartin, 29, 37, 51, 77, 111, 134, 146
Charles II, 74
Chandragupta Maurya, 27, 28, 134
Cis-Sutlej tribes, the, 106, 107, 115
Clive, 103
Cockell, William, 80, 82–3, 85–8
Crystal Palace, 136, 138–9

DALHOUSIE, annexes Punjab, 125; claims Koh-i-noor for Great Britain, 126–30; takes Koh-i-noor to Bombay, 133; refutes curse on Koh-i-noor, 142–3; comments on Koh-i-noor, 144–5, 151; cause of problem of ownership, 148–9
Darya-i-noor, compared with Koh-i-noor, 64
Dasyus, the, 22, 24, 134
Dawn, 16, 23, 134
Delhi, Turkish Sultanate of, 38, 42; conquered by Babur, 42, 44; 46, 77, 87; as Shahjahanabad, 54, 60, 66, 84; sacked by Wadir Shah, 85–6; occupied by Ahmad Shah Durrani, 94–5; occupied by Mahrattas, 104; 106, 127; Grand Durbar at, 146
Dhulip Singh, birth, 106; becomes Maharajah of Punjab, 122; treaty imposed on him by British, 126–7; sees Koh-i-noor again, 144–5; put forward as owner of diamond, 148; pleads for restitution, 149; 150
Din-i-Illahi, 49, 100
Dost Mohammed, 98, 116
Durranis, 93, 96–9, 113–15

EAST INDIA COMPANY, THE, launching of Indian voyages, 68–70; striking aspects of the company, 70; the company in India, 71–5; company comments on Nadir Shah, 80 et seq.; after Plassey, 104; increasing area of rule, 115, 122, 126; does not, however, gain Koh-i-noor, 126–7; presents Koh-i-noor to Queen Victoria, 138; 148
Eden, Miss Emily, 116, 117, 119
Elphinstone, Mountstuart, 108, 118

FARGHANA, 39, 40
Fath Ali Khan, 79, 81
Fathepur Sikri, 48, 50, 139

GENGHIS KHAN, 39, 82
Gita Govinda, 15
Goa, 56, 57, 73
Golkonda, 53, 60, 61
Govind, 10th guru of the Sikhs, 100, 101
Great Exhibiton, The, 136–40, 145
'Great Mogul' diamond, the, presented to Shah Jahan by Mir Jumla, 53; cut by Borgio and seen by Tavernier, 62; problem of identity of the three great diamonds, 62–4; cutting compared with Voorsanger's operation, 144
Gujerat, battle of, 123–4, 126, 148

HARAPPA, ancient twin capital of Indus valley, 22
Harappans, 134
Hinduism, 15, 25, 37
Hindu Kush, 93
Hiuen Tsiang, 33
Humayun, 42–3, 45–6, 50, 147

IBRAHIM LODI, 42–4, 73
Indus Valley Civilization, 22
Indra, Aryan Thunder-god, 22
Isfahan, 79, 81
Islam, 37–8, 49, 93

JAHANGIR (the 'World-Grasper'), 51, 71, 72, 74, 75
James I and VI, 68, 69, 73
Jizya, tax on non-Moslems, 48, 76

KABUL, 38, 39, 41–3, 84, 93, 94, 98, 99, 109, 114, 118, 119

Kandahar, 82, 83, 84, 114, 117, 118
Karnal, Battle of, 84–5
Karim Khan, 90–1
Kashmir, 98–9, 109
Kauravas, The, 25–6, 29
Khalsa, The, 101, 105, 107, 122, 149
Kharak Singh, son of Ranjit Singh, 105, 121, 148
Khorasan, 78–80, 91
Koh-i-noor, prehistory, 15–16, 25; comparison with 'Babur's diamond', 43; and with 'Great Mogul', 62–4; 70, 76–7; Nadir Shah takes and names it, 86–7; curse attending it, 89, 142–3; 90; and Shah Rukh Mirza and Agha Mohammed Khan, 92; hidden by Zaman Shah, 97; with Shah Shuja, 108; Ranjit Singh claims it, 109; Osborne describes it, 110; Beli Ram prevents it from being given away, 112; 113–15; surrendered to British, 125–8; almost lost, 129–30; leaves India, 130–4; 135; brought to England, 137; presented to Victoria, 138; exhibited (the 'Great Dimun'), 139–42; value of, 143; cut by Voorsanger, 144; Dhulip Singh sees it again, 145; problem of ownership, 147–51
Kollur, the mine where the Koh-i-noor was found, 58–60, 62
Krishna, 15, 17–21, 25–6

LAHORE, 84, 99–100, 103, 108, 109, 113, 122, 130, 133, 148–50
Lawrence, Henry, 125, 127–9
Lawrence, John, 127–30, 133
Login, Dr John, 128, 129, 144, 145
Ludhiana, 98, 113–15
Lytton, Lord, Viceroy of India, 146

MADRAS, 74, 75
Mahabharata, The, 25, 29
Mahmud of Ghazni, 37, 38, 94, 123
Mahrattas, The, 73–5, 103–5
Malik Mahmud, 80
Mansel, G. C., 128
Mauryans, The, 27, 37, 46
Medea, H.M.S., 133–4, 137–8
Megasthenes, 28
Methold, William, 58
Mir Jumla, 52, 53, 60, 63, 64, 144
Misr Beli Ram, 112, 128

INDEX

Moguls, The: founding of Empire, 41–5; its growth, 46–53; receive Koh-i-noor, 53; its new capital, 54; relations with East India Company, 71–4; Madras, Bombay, Calcutta, 74–5; autocracy as downfall, 76–7; defeated by Nadir Shah, 83–6; lose Koh-i-noor, 87; defeated by Ahmad Shah Durrani, 94; eighteenth-century decline, 103–4, 115
Mohammed Shah, 85–7
Mohenjo-Daro, ancient twin capital of Indus Valley, 22
Mulraj, 122, 123
Multan, 119–23
Myth of the diamond, 25–6, 29–33

NADIR SHAH, birth, 78; as general, 80–1; takes Persian throne, 82–3; invades India, 84; captures and sacks Delhi, 85–6; takes and names Koh-i-noor, 87; is assassinated, 88; events after his death, 89–90; 94, 101, 104, 115, 134, 142
Nanak, 1st guru of the Sikhs, 100–1

OSBORNE, WILLIAM, 110–12, 116

PAKISTAN, 150
Pandavas, 25, 29
Peacock Throne, 65, 86
Persia, 78–9, 81–3, 86, 90–2, 97, 150
Peshawar, 108, 116
Piyadisi (Asoka), 32
Porus, 26–7, 134
Prasena, 18, 21
Punjab, 94, 102–6, 121–2, 124–5, 127
Pushtunistan, 93–6

RAHDA, 15
Ramayana, The, 25
Rammalakota, 59
Ranjit Singh, Lion of the Punjab, physical appearance, 102; early life, 102–5; birth of 'son', Dhulip Singh, 106; Cis-Sutlej wars, 106–7; relations with British, 107, 115–16; rescues Shah Shuja and gains Koh-i-noor, 108–10; shows it to Osborne, 110–11; dies, 112; and Shah Shuja, 113–14; 119, 121–3, 134, 142–3
'Ratnins', the jewel of court, 30

SAMARKAND, 39, 40
Satrajit, 16–19, 21, 26
Savafids, 78, 79, 81
Seven Gems of the Universal Emperor, 29, 30
Shah Jahan, 51–2, 62, 71, 73–5, 85–6, 89
Shahjahanabad, 54, 60, 66
Shah Rukh Mirza, 90–2, 98
Shah Shuja, 96–9, 107; wears Koh-i-noor, 108; gives it up to Ranjit Singh, 109; 110, 111; escapes from prison, 113; in Ludhiana, 113–14; replaced on Afghan throne, 115–18; assassinated, 119; his valuation of the Koh-i-noor, 143
Shiites, 38, 45, 49
Sikhs, 94, 100–5, 107–10, 122–5, 127
Siva, 24
Sivaji Raja, 73–5, 77
Sleeman, Lt.-Col., 97, 130
Smith, Bosworth, 129, 133
Streeter, Edwin, 63
Sunnites, 38, 49
Surat, Battle of, 72–5
Surya, Aryan Sun-god, 16–17, 23, 26
Syamantaka, legendary original of Koh-i-noor, 16–22, 26

'Ta Indika', 28
Taj Mahal, 52
Tamerlane, 39, 41, 82, 85, 123
Tavernier, Jean-Baptiste: and Bernier, 52; in India, 54–61; sees 'Great Mogul' diamond, 62; his record of it, 62–4; and the Peacock Throne, 65–6; his later life and mysterious death, 66–7; 71, 76, 130
Taylor, Sergeant-Major, 117, 118
Thugs, 130–3
Tokmakof, 67
Trade's Increase, East India Company ship, 64, 69
'Triratna', the three jewels of Buddhism, 31

UNIVERSAL EMPEROR, 29–30, 134, 146
Ushas, Aryan goddess of the dawn, 16

VASCO DA GAMA, 55, 56
Vedas, The, 15, 22
Victoria, Princess, 150–1
Victoria, Queen, 62, 129, 130; and the Great Exhibition, 135–7, 139–43; shows diamond to Dhulip Singh, 145; becomes Empress of India, 146; 147–51

Vigne, 98–9, 113, 151
Vishnu, 24
Vishnu Purana, The, 15
Voorsanger (cutter of Koh-i-noor), 144

WATERFIELD, PRIVATE WILLIAM, 120–4
Wellesley, Lord, Governor-General, 104

YADAVAS, THE, 18–19, 29
Yudhisthira, 25, 26

ZAMAN SHAH, 96; imprisoned, blinded, hides Koh-i-noor, 97–9; his invasions of India, 102–3, 106; escapes to Punjab, 108